Carlton Dawe

The Emu's Head

Vol. 2

Carlton Dawe

The Emu's Head
Vol. 2

ISBN/EAN: 9783337729707

Printed in Europe, USA, Canada, Australia, Japan

Cover: Foto ©Thomas Meinert / pixelio.de

More available books at **www.hansebooks.com**

THE EMU'S HEAD

A Chronicle of Dead Man's Flat

W. CARLTON DAWE

AUTHOR OF
"MOUNT DESOLATION" "THE GOLDEN LAKE" ETC

IN TWO VOLUMES

VOL. II.

LONDON
WARD & DOWNEY
12 YORK STREET COVENT GARDEN
1893.

TO
MY FRIEND,
JOHN STEWART, Esq.,
OF
MELBOURNE, AUSTRALIA,
THIS BOOK IS INSCRIBED IN TOKEN
OF
THE MEMORY OF OLD DAYS.

CONTENTS.

CHAP.		PAGE
I.—Mr. Logan's Solicitude		1
II.—Delilah		22
III.—Husband and Wife		41
IV.—Gone!		59
V.—The Redemption of Kitty		84
VI.—Delilah Pays		110
VII.—The Cipher		132
VIII.—Morgan's Last Jaunt		159
IX.—Hall's Plant		179
X.—Into the Great Beyond		201
XI.—Which Concludes the Chronicle		215

THE EMU'S HEAD.
A Chronicle of Dead Man's Flat.

CHAPTER I.

MR. LOGAN'S SOLICITUDE.

In the afternoon Kitty appeared, having passed through a night more wretched than any she had ever known. Her eyes were red and swollen, her cheeks puffed; indeed her whole face bore a look of indescribable misery. She returned her estimable husband's salutations with a cold stare, and when he upbraided her for her unwifely spirit she told him to go and mind his own business. And away he went, thinking much of the strangeness which had come upon her, and wondering what quantity of truth the statement of Mr. Smith contained. That Kitty had liked George he was well aware, but that there was anything serious in that liking he never for one moment imagined, for to him she was a woman so proud that he did not fear she would condescend to stoop to any unworthy act. Yet he had determined to test her. Smith had asserted that a jealous woman would stop at nothing. Well, he would see. If her jealousy served his turn he might find it in his heart to forgive even her falseness. Yet, truth to tell, he did not glow with hope; though, knowing her impulsiveness, he did not doubt that once the idea got the mastery over her it would sweep away all opposition. If he could only corrupt her sufficiently he knew that victory was assured.

And all this time the object of his thoughts went on with her work, mute, unless it was to snap. That her thoughts were anywhere but with her beer-taps the least observant of her patrons could see; that there was some trouble in her heart, some pain-giving thought in her mind, all who took the trouble to look at her (and there are few men who would not have done so) felt assured. Consequently the inquiries respecting the state of her health were numerous, but these, instead of soothing her vanity, sounded like so many impertinences and but aggravated her the more, so that she was not a little relieved when Edith came to announce that tea was ready.

The young girl slipped an arm round her cousin's waist and kissed her.

"I was afraid you were very ill, dear," she said, "and I wanten so much to come to you. But do you know, Kitty, I was really afraid."

"Were you really?"

"Was it not silly of me? But you are better now, dear?

"Oh, yes. It was merely a headache."

"Why did you not come to me last night?" asked the girl. "I had so much to tell you."

"It was rather late when I went to bed. I was afraid of disturbing your—dreams."

The girl raised her cousin's hand to her lips and kissed it. Kitty winced, and made a pretence of drawing it away, and yet she could not. So hand in hand they entered the little sitting-room, and Kitty, seating herself at the head of the table, began to pour out the tea.

"Now," she cried, in a tone of affected gaiety, "tell me the news. All you were to have told me last night."

"Well," said the girl, blushing deeply, "George—that is, Mr. Vincent——"

"Oh, call him George," laughed Kitty, coldly, "we all do."

"George has asked me to marry him."

Kitty winced again, the action making

her spill some of the tea on the nice clean cloth, but she replied without raising her eyes, "And you, I presume, said 'Yes'?"

The girl bowed her head.

For a moment or two there was a deep, oppressive silence between the two women. Kitty stirred her tea quietly, staring into the cup as though it possessed some magnetic attraction.

"Well, I hope you will be happy," she said at last. "George told me all about it last night. You think you like him?"

"Oh, Kitty, I love him, or I should never think of marrying him."

"That, at least, is extremely satisfactory. But tell me, Edie, dear—for you know I am both cousin and guardian, and must therefore take a practical view of the case—how does he propose to keep you?"

"I'm sure I don't know," replied the girl, looking quite crestfallen. "I never thought of that."

"You can't live on love, you know," laughed Kitty coldly.

"He is strong—he can work," began the girl.

"No doubt—but you don't want to live in a canvas tent down the creek? I'm afraid you would find it even more trying than the bar. But there, I suppose George has a tidy little sum saved up?"

"He had some I know, but it was stolen last night."

"Stolen! How was that?"

"Some robbers broke into his tent, rifled his box and carried off a lot of gold. But he doesn't mind that, for he'll be rich pres——" She pulled up quickly, remembering that she was stepping upon forbidden ground, and blushed. This sudden stoppage and confusion did not escape Mrs. Logan.

"How—rich? What do you mean by that?" she asked. But Edith only blushed more, looking more confused. "Is it a secret between you?" The girl bowed her head. "Oh, very well, then, don't divulge it for the world."

"You are not angry, dear? It was his wish."

"Not I, indeed. Of what consequence is it to me one way or the other?"

Before Edith could reply, and to her inexpressible relief, a gentle tap was heard at the door and Mr. Logan entered, a winning smile on his fat face.

"May I be permitted to indulge in a little light refreshment?" he asked, pointing his fat forefinger at the teapot.

Kitty looked at him sullenly. Then she said, "You may, if you don't mind putting on your coat."

"Coat," said Logan with a smile, "I'm much more comfortable as I am."

"No doubt."

"Well, upon my soul, Kit, you're a cool one. No one would ever think that you had seen your father carving the Sunday dinner in his shirt-sleeves."

"I had no authority over my father," she said, the blood rushing in darker torrents to her already flushed face. "Besides, he was not a gentleman like you."

"I shouldn't think he was," grinned her spouse. "Fancy old Tom being a gentleman. Oh, it's too funny, Kit, it is reelly." And, laughing heartily, the worthy landlord waddled off in the direction of the bar, returning a moment or two after with his coat on.

"There," he said, "I suppose you think I'm a gentleman now?"

"Do you think I'm a fool?"

"I think she's in a precious bad humour, don't you, Edith?"

"She has been very unwell," replied the girl.

"Poor old Kit. The diggings a bit too hard for you, eh? Well, when we've made our pile we'll pack up, go down to Melbourne and buy a house at St. Kilda. Or, if you like, we'll take a trip to England. I've often thought I should like to take a run over and have a look at that blooming country. It would be mighty interesting to see the place which produced Dick Turpin and Jack Sheppard."

"They are not the only great men it has produced," said his wife severely.

"That's true enough. There's Blueskin, and Jonathan Wild, and Claude Duval—and heaps of 'em. Ah, take my word for it, England's a great country." And as if to further emphasise this statement he lifted the little cup to his lips, and solemnly swallowed its contents. At the same moment Edith caught his eye, and, acting on the suggestion which sparkled therein, rose and quitted the room.

For quite five minutes husband and wife sat without uttering a word, she evidently occupied with a series of none too agreeable thoughts, he alternately sipping the tea and watching her. Presently he spoke.

"When do the young people propose to marry?"

She looked blankly up from her reverie. He repeated the question.

"I don't know," she answered shortly.

"You know, he's a lucky dog," continued Mr. Logan with a soft chuckle, which might mean either of two things;—satisfaction at her tone and demeanour, or at the prospect of the youthful alliance, "an exceedingly lucky dog. Why, there's not a man on the Flat who wouldn't spread his gold-dust beneath her feet if she'd only look at him. And some of them have got it pretty thick in their pockets, too, I can tell you. I suppose she's clean gone on him?"

"No doubt."

"And he on her?"

"No doubt."

"My pal Smith was, but then he always had a weakness for the women. Not that he's any great chop in the beauty line; but I'm told they like 'em ugly."

"Then you ought to be in great demand."

"I didn't say I wasn't," he replied with a knowing smile. "But you don't expect a fellow to blow his own trumpet, do you? Modest is as modest does, Mrs. Logan."

"And to what does all this modesty tend?" she asked coldly.

"'Gad, you're as cutting as a hailstorm, Kit; but you're a sensible woman for all that. Now what's your candid opinion of this marriage?"

"My opinion," she laughed a little excitedly. "What is it to do with me? If they have determined to marry, what earthly power can stop them?"

"Marriages have been stopped, you know," suggested her husband in a low, meaning voice. "And, between ourselves, Kit, I think we ought to try and stop this one."

"Why should we?" she asked, turning her searching eyes full on his face.

"My dear Kit, we can't let the girl marry a pauper."

She laughed oddly. "You have grown mightily interested all at once."

"I am growing fond of the child. But is my interest in this business stronger than yours?"

"I'm afraid I do not quite understand you," she said coldly, for there had been a certain insinuating ring in Mr. Logan's voice which had not entirely escaped her.

"Ought it to be stronger?" he asked, this time with a frankness which was charming. "You are the girl's cousin, guardian, only friend. You really must not allow her to throw herself away on a digger-chap—a fellow who hasn't a pound-note to his name."

"But he can work, and he will make money. Only this moment she told me some nonsense about his being on the road to fortune."

"Not such nonsense either, Kit, take my word for it. It's a fortune of twenty-five thousand pound. Once he gets it, the wedding's a moral."

"Well, and why not?" Her voice was cold and low, but her eyes belied her tone, and Mr. Logan, who was not ignorant of nature's writings, read the lines quite easily.

"Because, Kit," he said slowly, "I'm not altogether sure that Vincent would make the girl a proper husband. You see, his morals are a bit off, and the idea of entrusting one who has twined herself about my lonely heart"—here he looked reproachfully at his wife—" to a fellow of no moral principle, goes clean against the grain.

Besides, Kit," he asked with no little dignity, "how could I allow my wife's cousin to go and live in a hut at the camp?"

"But since your wife's cousin is a woman and her own mistress, I should like to know how you propose preventing her doing what she wishes?"

"If you wouldn't mind trying to ask a question without sneering, I wouldn't mind telling you a very effi—what's that blooming word?—a very good way of doing it. In the first place, Vincent has no money."

"Granted."

"Then it must also be granted that we cannot allow our dear cousin to mate herself with a pauper. The man who marries her must be able to keep her in a manner befitting her station."

"What nonsense," said his wife.

He smiled with his funny little eyes. "Will he think so? Will she?"

"But what about this fortune — this

twenty-five thousand pounds? A man with such a sum as that, or even with the prospect of it, cannot very well be set down as a pauper."

"Now that's argument, Kitty," said her husband admiringly, "that's the head that won my heart in the old Bunyip days." Kitty winced, as she always did at the mention of that fatal period. The word Bunyip referred to the name of her father's hotel—a memory of the most painful nature.

"Ah, they were happy times, Kit," he went on, perhaps not altogether unconscious of the irritation he caused her, "such times as I shall never see again. You were as sprightly as a kangaroo rat in those days, and had a face as bright and cheerful as a bit of new pewter. And look at you now. You've never got a pleasant word for me, and your face is as black and glum as a pot of stale porter. When I think of what you are to me, and what you were when we went away to Geelong for our honeymoon, I feel as though I could lie down and die." And though Mr. Logan did not exactly suit the action to the word, he nevertheless blinked his eyes in the most remarkable manner, and wobbled on his seat like a sympathetic jelly-fish.

Kitty's brows drew close together, and her beautiful full mouth curled up contemptuously. It was evident that she did not appreciate her husband's eloquent outburst.

"You will be good enough to stop that drivel," she said, "if you wish me to listen. Moreover, I have no wish to be reminded of what I am eternally striving to forget."

"Well, you take it, Mrs. Logan. Anybody would think you wasn't proud of the name you bore."

She laughed disdainfully. "I ought to be."

". Yes," said he impressively, though his little eyes shone angrily through their ridges of fat, "you ought. It's a good name and an honest one, and belonged to the kings of Ireland, too."

"I never knew an Irish name that didn't."

"Nor I," replied her husband with a laugh, "which is more than you can say for the English, anyway. But you were suggesting that George Vincent could not be poor with the almost certain prospect of getting twenty-five thousand pound. No more he could. But if by any chance he should lose that prospect?"

"Well, suppose he did?" Her voice quivered in spite of her determination.

"Not that I hope he will," added Logan, "for you can easily overlook a man's morals when he heaps twenty-five thousand pound beside 'em."

"This is supposing he gets the fortune?"

"He's sure to get it—unless he loses the paper," the man added indifferently.

"The paper—what paper?"

"It's a bit of paper written in cipher. It tells where the twenty-five thousand pound is hid."

"You don't mean Ben Hall's Plant?"

"Yes, my girl, I believe that is what they call it. I wish I only had his chance. I'd settle ten thousand on you, Kit, that's what I'd do, and you shouldn't live with me, old girl, unless you liked. But of course, they'll get it instead. George will pack up his swag and toddle off to Melbourne, buy a villa at the seaside—though I wouldn't mind Collingwood Flat with such a girl—become a regular toff, and forget that there was ever such a place as Dead Man's Flat."

"Does he know you know he has this paper?"

Mr. Logan felt his blood thrill, but

masking his delight answered indifferently, "Bless you no. He thinks we're as green as he pretends to be."

"Then how did you know it was in his possession?"

Peter was a little taken aback at this question, but cocking up his head like a dog, he said with a tantalising smile, "How do I know that he carries it in his waist-belt? Never you mind, my dear. It's a secret between me and the little bird that brought it." And with the same tantalising look on his face he wagged his head sagaciously, rose from his seat, and waddled from the room. Once outside the door, he stopped for a few moments listening intently, then going down on his knees, an elephantine movement, but one which he accomplished noiselessly, he peeped through the keyhole. One quick glance seemed sufficient. Arising with a look of intense satisfaction on his ugly face he waddled towards the bar, muttering, "The devil's got her fast, we'll have some fun by-and-by."

For a long time after her worthy spouse had quitted the apartment Kitty sat with her cheek in her hand, a prey to a thousand racking thoughts. Her husband's insinuations had found a ready entrance into her breast, whence they issued to her brain, blurring her sense of honour and self-respect. Now was she equal to any undertaking, no matter how despicable or daring; and now again the softer and purer side of her nature would uprise and drive back the legions of false and foul thoughts which encompassed her. Passionate and wilful by nature, ill-trained; brought up by a father more passionate and ill-trained than herself, it is not surprising that she should have been one whose life was a constant rebellion against restraint. Neither is the atmosphere of the bar-room one in which such natures imbibe humility, the meekness of the dove. Ever since she was old enough to be noticed she was praised for her beauty; as a woman, flattery rang incessantly in her ears; when she spoke it was to be obeyed, when her beautiful mouth curled in anger, men shrank back as they would from a scourge. But she was proud, proud as Lucifer; a vain and ignorant pride to be sure—devilish, obstinate as death. With proper training she would have been a grand and stately lady, one in whom all people would have seen that curious phenomenon known only to the initiated—the mark of noble birth. You see it in queens and their satellites, but never in the thousands of beautiful stars which illumine this earth with their glory. If ever there was a star-woman it was this daughter of the tap-room. Beautiful, inscrutable; like a star in brightness, indifference; but most like a star in her fire.

CHAPTER II.

DELILAH.

ALL the next morning Kitty went about with a strange haunted look in her eyes. Her husband's veiled suggestions had found a ready road to her envious heart, and though at times her sense of honour shrank from subterfuge or deceit, her passionate nature revolted at the thought of a tame submission. To her it seemed no wrong that she should envy her cousin the love of this young man, for was she not loveless and more miserable than any woman beneath the sun? She was not a false woman; she had not sought him. He came bringing sunshine into her life, and she dreaded the threatening gloom. It was death to her, and who loves death so well that he will not part with it? Her sense, it is true, strove hard with her desire. She knew she had no right to look upon this young man; knew that her very hope, if gratified, would bear an everlasting anguish. And yet she could not help but look. How many of us, O my brothers and sisters, know nothing of this longing?

Once only Edith spoke to her that day, and when she kissed her lips she found them cold and hard. Glancing up into her cousin's eyes she was terrified at the look she saw. If eyes can devour, and we have often read of them doing so, Kitty's were certainly feasting gluttonously on the girl's face. There was a look of wonder, of yearning, and trying-to-see. She held Edith's head between her hands and stared into her face with an intenseness almost terrifying; every hair of that pretty head she took in, every feature, every curve. Then with an odd little laugh she turned aside, while the girl, more than fearful, hurried off to her room, convinced that her cousin had gone mad.

There was still another member of this strange household to whom the eccentricities of Mrs. Kitty seemed to afford no end of speculation. Mr. Logan watched her all through that morning with unremitting zeal, satisfied, yet furious. That his seeds of suggestion had not fallen on barren ground, his wife's pre-occupied air and eccentricity of manner fully justified him in believing, which, though undoubtedly gratifying, was none the less exceedingly provoking, for to him it proved conclusively that her affections were lavished on another. Now Mr. Logan was not one of those whom we could call extremely fastidious, but even the most depraved of mortals have feelings, and sentiments too, when their own skin is in danger, and if this vulgar creature had ever loved anything it was himself. And if we go still further and admit that there is a universal similarity in human nature, we shall understand why he fumed so boisterously at the better half of himself turning its back, as it were, upon himself. In other words, the worthy landlord was jealous. He had taken this girl to his bosom (in a moment of weakness it is true), and once a man has done that sort of thing he cannot altogether forget what has been. He may hate her, despise her, wish her to the devil every hour of his life; but he can never forget that she is and has been a wife to him, and that fact alone will make her different from all other women. Now the excellent Boniface could do much to suit his ends, as we have seen, and shall see more; he would have objected to very little, by way of experiment, but that she should, virgin-like, lock herself against him while her whole soul yearned for another, was what no reputable husband could be expected to tolerate. Neither would he—he'd see them dashed first. I am afraid, though, that he did not confine himself to this simple epithet. At times the most desperate resolves whirled through his brain, and if only one or two of them had been put into execution it would have gone hard with Mr. George Vincent. But luckily for that young man, Mr. Logan had some solid reasons for not appearing himself upon the scene of any action which might lead to an investigation; besides which, was it not a much more clever and palatable thing to play off the woman against her lover? Once let the young man know what Kitty really was, and there would be no more to fear from him. And as the landlord watched his wife from out the corners of his little eyes, marked the gloom of her brow, the sullen light in her eyes, he felt as though he were indeed two persons, one half of him being full of hate, the other of joy.

In the afternoon Kitty went out alone, an unusual occurrence, and one which made poor Edith feel exceedingly miserable; but Mr. Logan, who watched his wife sail forth, went back to his cigar with a grim smile, and for the rest of that afternoon proved himself the jolliest landlord imaginable. He did not see her on her return, but when she appeared in the bar that night, he marked her altered looks and wondered much what she had done or was doing. In an aimless way she attended to her duties, acknowledged the many salutations with a stiff bow or a vacant look, and on more than one occasion astonished her interrogators by replying to their queries in a way they little expected. But about half-past eight Vincent entered. At his approach she began to tremble violently, and her pale face flushed crimson, but with one of those great efforts, of which only such natures as hers are capable, she repressed the strange quivering in her breast, gulped down the lump that rose in her throat.

"Ah, Mrs. Kitty," he cried, extending his hand, his face aglow with life and hope, "how is the world using you?"

"Pretty much the same," she said, looking into his happy face, and thinking she had never seen more fearless eyes, a more manly-looking man.

"And what may that be?"

"Not worth the trouble of talking about," she said a little wearily. "But you look the picture of impudent health."

"And I am impudent. Do you know, I carry my head like a drum-major and strut like a turkey-cock. When I walk the ground seems elastic, and there isn't a man on the Flat I couldn't knock out inside of five rounds."

"You are light-headed, George."

"Yes. I must be very careful or I shall go off like a balloon. But where is she?"

"She?"

"You know." He smiled in a sheepish sort of way, just like a big, overgrown boy. The corners of Kitty's mouth dropped, but she nodded towards the private parlour and he disappeared with alacrity.

What her feelings were during the next two hours of courtship it might not be very difficult to imagine if we set ourselves the task. All through that period, which seemed like an eternity, she paced the limits of her bar mechanically, smiling, talking, working—yet, above all, thinking, thinking, till her poor brain reeled. And, as there are no limits to imagination, it may easily be conceived that the brain drove many a shudder in upon the heart, and that despair, like the upas, sprang up, a darksome growth. And during the whole of this time her worthy spouse, in his shirt-sleeves, lounged in his favourite corner of the bar, smoked strong cigars, and drank enormous quantities of rum. And his little eyes beamed like newly-polished beads, and his fat cheeks curled up about his eyes in the most singular manner, and his fat fingers, on which glistened three beautiful diamond rings of doubtful value, twined themselves lovingly around each other, or patted with brotherly solicitude the backs of his fat hands. An exceedingly sociable Boniface was Mr. Logan that night—one who would have stood his worst enemy a drink, or kissed his mother-in-law.

It must have been quite half-past ten, if not later, when Mr. Vincent emerged from the sacred precincts of the "private parlour" and appeared in the little snuggery at the back of the bar. His face was flushed, his eyes radiant with joy; indeed, so happy did he look that poor Kitty was forced to the subterfuge of wiping her mouth, in order to hide the quiver of her lips.

"Well," she said, with a strange, excited little laugh, "is it still such a serious matter?"

"Still," he repeated. "It's more serious than ever."

"And the happy day is fixed?"

"No—not exactly. The fact of the matter is this. As yet I'm scarcely in a position to set up housekeeping."

"But you soon hope to be? she asked naïvely.

"It will not be longer than I can help, you may be sure."

"But is not gold-digging a very uncertain business, and may you not work for years without striking a patch?"

"I shall not."

"You are not wanting in confidence."

"I think I have a right to feel confident, Mrs. Kitty. I will tell you all about it some day—say when you come down to Melbourne to stay with Edith and me."

"You are very kind." Her beautiful mouth quivered painfully, and once more her handkerchief was brought into requisition.

"You say it as though you hardly meant it," he said.

"Do I? What makes you think that?" Her eyes sought his full of fire and pain. He turned his face away, feeling quite embarrassed.

"I don't know," he said with an awkward laugh. "I suppose I'm a bit of a fool. But, by Jove! there goes eleven. I must be off, Mrs. Kitty."

"Wait a moment," she said, somewhat hastily, nervously; "you were not always in such a hurry. Besides, George,

I want to drink success to your engagement."

"Your wish is a command, Mrs. Kitty. You always were a queen, you know."

"Yes," she exclaimed bitterly, "of the tap-room. But you must give up paying those foolish compliments now—they may be misunderstood. Besides, George, if you only knew how bitter they taste, how sarcastic they sound, you would spare me. They are all very well from the others, they have neither taste nor sound then, but from you they are more than cruel."

"I never meant that they should be so," he said. "Believe me, I never meant that."

"I know it, and that is why it pains me so. But go into the little parlour, the one you have just vacated—if you can tolerate it without a certain presence. I will be with you in a moment."

Vincent passed out from the little room and

entered again the chamber in which he had but lately dreamt away two of the sweetest hours he had ever known. Even now the memory of her presence seemed to fill the room with an indescribable sweetness, and he wafted a sigh to her and a silent prayer that all good spirits might protect her. Presently he was joined by Kitty, who bore on a tray two glasses of champagne and a half-empty bottle of the same sparkling wine. The tray she deposited carefully on the table, handed Vincent one of the glasses, and took the other one herself.

"Long life and happiness," she said, raising the glass to her lips, though her hand shook slightly as she did so, "may you both know all imaginable joy," and she tossed off the bubbling liquor.

"Thank you, Mrs. Kitty," he said looking up into her face in his frank, strange way, "thank you a thousand times. May no cloud ever come to darken the glory of our friendship." He raised his glass as he spoke.

"Stop!" she cried suddenly, "I—I——"

"What is the matter?"

She hid her confusion by pouring out another glass of wine. She put her teeth together and clenched the bottle till her finger tips seemed bursting; then looking into his face with a strangely-pathetic smile she said:

"Stop—stop till I say Amen to that wish."

He smiled and drained his glass; she did the same. He then took out his pipe and began filling it preparatory to his setting forth, and while he did so she sat watching him, her face almost ghastly in its terror, her eyes shining like two supernatural lights. Suddenly glancing up he caught that awful look of anguish, and asked her what she meant by staring at him in that uncanny fashion; but she only laughed nervously, being too frightened to speak.

All at once George gave a dreadful yawn.

"Pardon me, Mrs. Kitty," he said as soon as he regained control of his jaws, "but I feel most infernally sleepy. I think I had better be up and going. Can't understand it," he continued, trying hard to stifle another tremendous yawn, "can't for the life of me. So awfully sudden, too." And leaning back on the sofa he re-commenced to yawn in a truly disgraceful manner.

"You must be very tired," said Kitty. "Lie back and take a little nap. I'll wake you before we close." Saying which she took up the tray and glasses and disappeared.

George, looking up and finding her gone, attempted to rise from the sofa, but his knees refusing to bear him he fell back with a sigh. One feeble effort he made against the demon exhaustion, then closed his eyes and was soon breathing the loud, regular breath of the heavy sleeper.

With a noiseless tread, and a ghastly, haunted face, and eyes that shone with a fearful radiance, Kitty stole guiltily into the room, and with never a sound advanced to the couch on which her victim lay. He breathed hard, his chest rising and falling with a troubled motion, while his face had an unusual flush upon it. For a full minute she stood over him, the unenviable possessor of a world of maddening thoughts. Now her purpose cooled, now it flared up again like fire ; now she hid her face in her hands with shame, and now the evil which was in her urged her on with many a taunt.

"It is a fair battle," it whispered; " do—do!"

A dozen times she was on the point of relinquishing the struggle, a dozen times she turned her face to the door, as if to go; but again came the evil whisper and the jealous thoughts, and her eyes encountering his flushed face, her better purpose wavered.

"My darling, oh, my darling," she muttered, and sinking to her knees beside him she pressed his head passionately to her breast and kissed him as though the whole world hung on his lips.

"Darling, darling," she cooed, softly as a fond mother might to a sleeping babe, "I cannot part with you, oh, I cannot part with you, darling, darling."

And the flush deepened on his face, and he put his arms about her neck, and drew her face down to him and kissed her, too, as though the whole world hung on her lips. And still in her paradise was the trail of the serpent, for amid his kisses he had muttered a name—not hers. With a shudder and a half-stifled moan she withdrew from his embrace and hid her face in her hands.

And then began that business which shrivelled every atom of her soul and made her feel sick with shame and guilt. Setting her quivering lips together, and trying to forget that every pulse throbbed "shame," that every vein in her body ran cold with horror, she deliberately searched his pockets for that paper which was to bring him fortune and her despair. With trembling fingers, with fingers which stung whenever they came in contact with any sort of paper, she went deftly through with her despicable task, but to her horror and joy discovered no sign of the document. And all the while her victim slept soundly on, a frank, boyish smile playing round the corners of his mouth.

But she had not forgotten the secret so

ingeniously disclosed by her husband, and having worked herself up to her present pitch of desperation, she knew that no greater degradation could befall her, no matter what she did. The iron came into her face, her beautiful mouth dropped, and with a sudden ferocity, and determination which had to be quickly executed lest it cooled, she turned to search his belt; and it so happened that the first little pouch she opened contained the treasure. Making sure that this scrap of yellow paper was the thing for which she had pledged her honour, she hastily slipped it into her bosom, re-arranged his attire, and then fled from the room.

CHAPTER III.

HUSBAND AND WIFE.

HALF an hour later George Vincent awoke with a sudden start, and for the moment seemed both surprised and confused at beholding Kitty before him.

"Where am I?" he asked, sitting up and staring round in a bewildered way. "You, Mrs. Kitty! Why, I thought I was in my bunk at the camp. How did I come here?"

"Well, that's a pretty question to ask me," she replied. "Have you been drinking very much to-day, George?"

"No—at least I have no recollection of so doing. And yet I feel as though I had," he continued, passing his parched tongue over his burning lips. "My mouth's as dry as dust."

"A touch of the sun," she said. "You had better go home and have a good night's rest. No — don't drink anything more to-night. You are much better without it."

"I think I will follow your maternal advice," he said with a laugh. "To tell you the truth, I feel quite done up. Hollo!" he exclaimed as he arose, "my knees seem precious weak. By Jove, I wonder if it is a touch of the sun?"

"I hope not. I daresay it is merely overwork and excitement."

"My dear Mrs. Kitty, you surely don't take me for a young lady, do you?" he cried, looking into her eyes with a frank and honest smile.

"I only wished to suggest a reason," she stammered; but she could neither look into his face nor smile honestly. She felt as though she would never smile again.

"Well," he said, "if it is sunstroke I hope you won't let them keep me in that zinc shanty on the hill. I was in it the other day and it was hot enough there to kill a black fellow."

"I can promise you the coolest room in the 'Emu's Head.'"

"Thank you," he said, "that is you all over. It's not for my sake, you know, that I dread the zinc hospital. It was quite good enough for me before, but now——"

"Yes, yes. I think, however, that you will find my suggestion the right one," she answered coldly, as she lead the way into the passage.

"I believe you," he replied, stamping his feet. "I feel stronger already." By this time the door was reached and opened.

"Good night, Mrs. Kitty."

"Good night, George."

A hearty grip of the hand, a grip that made her wince—it seemed so *honest*. For a moment she watched till his figure was lost in the darkness, then re-entered the house, closing and locking the door.

On the threshold of the room which she and Vincent had just vacated stood the podgy form of her husband, a wicked leer in his eye, a restlessness in his mien which was entirely foreign to his sluggish nature —at least most people would have thought so, though Mr. Peter Logan had seen some things which would have stirred the blood of the most phlegmatic Dutchman. He made way for his wife with an exaggerated bow, and as she entered the room shut the door quickly behind her.

"What did you do that for?" she asked, turning on him suspiciously.

"I want to have a little quiet talk with

you, my dear." He offered her a chair as he spoke—a piece of politeness which considerably startled her, not that he had never been polite, only of late he had been extremely remiss in the more delicate attentions.

"I cannot talk to-night—I am tired."

"So am I," and as if to prove the truth of this statement he stifled a huge yawn; "so am I, my dear," he continued, "but business first and pleasure afterwards has always been my motto."

"Well," she said, seeing that he was in one of his jocular moods, and knowing how devilish they were, "what is it?" And with a very poor grace she sat herself in the chair which he had so politely proffered.

He laughed. "You seem a bit out of sorts, my dear."

"What do you mean?" she asked, staring coldly at him.

"That's it," he grinned, "that's what I call the reel thing. The devil himself couldn't beat you at cheek."

"If you only mean to insult me," she cried, bounding to her feet.

"I have no such intention," he replied, "I want to be friends again."

Her lip curled scornfully. "That cannot be," she said. "I do not wish it."

"Yet you are my wife." She did not answer. "Well," he said, "we won't quarrel over that. Let us be friends if we cannot be man and wife."

"There is no reason why we should be enemies."

"None at all, Kit; so tell me, my dear, how you succeeded to-night."

"I—I don't understand you."

"I think you do." There was a cunning look on his vulgar face which made her shudder.

"Oh! very well then, I do." She threw

herself back in the chair with a look of careless defiance.

"Look here, Kit, why is it we can't try and sail smoothly, for a change?"

"I have no wish that we should not. You go your way, let me go mine, and we shall sail smoothly enough."

"I have no doubt, but the arrangement is impracticable. How can a man who is a man let his wife steer her own course?"

She laughed a low, mocking laugh. "Really, I thought you had forgotten you have a wife."

"No; but I don't think I have remembered it too soon."

She flushed painfully. "You are a scoundrel," she exclaimed hotly.

"I know it," answered her worthy spouse with an exquisite smile. "What are you?"

The question evoked such a horrible reply that she dared not give it utterance. Her proud defiant eyes fell before her husband's malevolent scrutiny. What was she? False woman, false wife, false friend. Yet she had much of good in her in spite of all, and that quality seemed but to accentuate her distress. She grew hot and cold by turns, and had a sympathetic friend been near her at that moment she would have poured into his or her ears the whole history of her woes. This feeling comes to us all at times, and there are moments in almost every life when confession is absolutely necessary, Hence the great power of the Romish Church. It supplies a human necessity in the confessional; for the many are weak of spirit, and it is an inestimable boon to such that they may pour their sorrows into sympathetic ears.

Had Mr. Peter Logan been a sympathetic man, and had he only seized his golden opportunity, there is no knowing what happiness might not have been in store for him; but, unfortunately, he was cast in an entirely different mould, and had no more fine feeling than one of his own pint pots.

"You don't answer me, Kit," he continued in his tantalising way. "Well, well, perhaps it's better not. I don't suppose I could twist much good out of it whatever you said. If you like we'll cry off. Only — only you must tell me how you succeeded."

"I do not know what you mean, and I have nothing to tell you."

He laughed roughly. "Don't you think it's time you dropped that tone? It riles a man when he knows all about your goings on. But there, there, I'm a peaceable man and of a forgiving nature. Give us the paper, Kit."

"The paper?" she repeated, like one trying to grasp his meaning.

"Yes," he said angrily, "the paper."

"I don't understand you."

"Don't lie, you faggot! I saw it all through the keyhole, kisses and all. Give us the paper."

"I haven't got it," she cried stubbornly.

When she resolved to plunder Vincent of his secret she had also determined that no one else should profit by it, and it must be added to her credit that no thought of enriching herself, in a monetary sense, had pervaded her mind during the planning of the outrage. That it might keep him from the arms of her rival was all the recompense she asked; for she had dreamt that the time might quickly come when she should be able to proclaim her freedom to the world. Then he might—he might. The thought humbled her dignity to the dust, but we doubt if there is not much more pleasure in humility, when congenial, than in any other state. Therefore she repeated stubbornly, "I haven't got it, I tell you, and I wouldn't give it to you if I had."

"Look here," said he, rising, his voice full of suppressed passion, his brow lowering like a thundercloud, "I have had about as much of your airs and tantrums as I intend to stand. You have treated me more like a dog than a man, and I'm about sick of it."

She tossed her head scornfully, the anger darting in little flashes from her eyes. "As you please. It concerns me nothing what you say or do. If I treat you as a dog, it is because I think you deserving of no better treatment."

"Yet you thought me good enough to marry."

"Did I? I am not aware that I ever told you so. If I did I unhesitatingly withdraw the statement."

"You married me anyway."

"You answered my purpose; you took

me from a home I detested. I went with the first man who asked me."

" You're a beauty, ain't you?"

" Now let us understand each other once for all. There can be no mincing of matters between us now. You must go your way, I mine. Under those conditions only can we live beneath the same roof."

" A mighty fine arrangement, no doubt, and one that would suit you admirably; but it won't do for me, Kitty Logan. I'm the master here, you hussy, lover or no lover, and I'll take good care that you shall know it too." He took a step towards her with his two hands clenched, a ferocious look on his ugly face. " If you value your skin, you traitress, give me that paper. I've promised you ten thousand, haven't I? It's a bargain between you and me. We need let no one else into the secret. If the money won't satisfy you, I'll clear, I will upon my soul, and you shall never see my face again." This inducement seeming to him of much importance, he emphasised it with due sincerity.

"I tell you I haven't got the paper," she said doggedly.

Mr. Logan growled out a terrible oath. "Why will you lie like that when I saw you search him?"

"I searched him I know," she replied in the same defiant tone, "but I saw nothing relating to a treasure."

"But you saw a piece of paper with some capital letters written on it which might have excited your curiosity?" he insinuated. "Come now, Kit, you've got the key of Ben's Plant. Hand it over."

"How did you know there was such a paper in existence?"

"Never you mind," he growled. "I did know—that's enough for you."

"Hardly. I should like to know how you came by this secret. Mr. Vincent has never spoken of it. How then could you connect him with it?"

"What the devil's that to do with you?" roared Logan furiously.

"Everything," she answered calmly. "To have known that Mr. Vincent held this secret you must previously have known the man whom he found murdered in Little Lonsdale Street."

Logan's fat face grew ghastly and he stepped back a pace or two as though driven by an unseen blow; but, his natural ferocity and impudence coming quickly to his rescue, he pulled himself up, as it were, and with clenched hands swung forward as if to strike her.

"What I know or don't know," he hissed, "Is nothing to you. If you take my advice you'll go about with your eyes shut. It's safest, wisest, best, you meddling fool. You've got a fortune in that paper, and I must have it."

"First tell me how you knew there was such a paper, if you did not know the man, Billy Jackson?"

He laughed. "There was a woman once whose curiosity caused her to look back. You know what became of her? Don't let your curiosity run away with your discretion. How I came to know the secret matters nothing to you."

"Perhaps not; but I should like to know who you are?"

"I am your husband. That should be enough for any honest woman."

"It should be; yet a woman's honesty cannot cover her husband's guilt. I should like to know if you were in Little Lonsdale Street that night when Mr. Vincent drove the cowardly murderers away from their unarmed victim."

"Look here," said Logan in a low, strained voice, a fearfully cruel look on his flabby face, "I want no more of your talk, no more of your damned insinuations, and I'll not stand 'em, d'ye hear, I'll not stand another word. Give us the paper and you may go to the devil if you choose."

"I tell you I have not the paper, and if I had I would not give it to you."

"You wouldn't, eh?" The hate in the man's eyes shone out most dreadfully, and he panted like one who breathes with difficulty.

"No, I would not." And very grand and beautiful she looked as she stood there defying him, her bold head thrown defiantly back, her proud lips curling contemptuously.

"Then take that!" he hissed, and drawing suddenly near he smote her a stinging blow on those proud lips with his open hand, cutting them on the teeth behind.

She staggered back like one thunderstruck, amazement on her face. For a moment she seemed almost paralysed, more with the wonder of the blow than the pain of it. But only for a moment. With a hoarse cry of passion and hate she seized a great lustre from off the mantelpiece and hurled it full at his face. But being fortunate enough to dodge it, he sprang at her before she could seize another missile and, catching her a vicious blow with his clenched fist, knocked her senseless.

"There," he exclaimed savagely, as he knelt beside her and eagerly began to open the bosom of her dress," I knew I should never get any good out of you till I had licked you. Pity I didn't do it long ago. Ah!" he ejaculated triumphantly as he drew forth the mystic paper, "you hadn't it, eh, you hussy, you hadn't it? There, take that for your airs and your tantrums, and for all you've made me suffer, and if it ain't good enough for you I'll give you plenty more for the asking." And with his open hand he smote her once more upon her bleeding mouth. She gave a long, low moaning cry and then lay still as death.

Mr. Logan arose to his feet with a look of the most intense satisfaction on his ugly face, turned out the light and quitted the apartment.

CHAPTER IV.

GONE!

GEORGE, in the meantime, was plodding his way towards the camp, striving with all the power of his intellect to account for the strange sleep and the stranger sensations which he now felt in every pulse of his body. He knew he had drunk nothing in quantities sufficiently large to affect him thus, and he imagined that he must either have caught a touch of the sun, or that excitement and overwork had wrought this surprising effect. He, however, revived in a wonderful manner as he tramped along; his brain grew clearer, his limbs stronger. The sweet night air sang blithely round his ears, and opening his mouth he inhaled it as though it were a draught of some delicious wine. And as his weakness wore off so faded his interest in its cause, and his mind became engrossed with thoughts of the sweet girl of whom he dreamt every night. What innumerable fond things were whispered in each other's ears that night it would become us not to say, merely for the gratification of excessive curiosity; but that they were very dear, and had wrought a great impression on the young man, there could be little doubt, for his blood began to glow as he conjured up the sweet scene, and in the sighings of the wind he thought he heard the murmur of her voice, and as the warm sweet breeze kissed his lips he shut his eyes and thought it was her breath.

Arriving at his tent he was greeted with a cheerful snore from his mate Phil; and here it may be said to that worthy's credit that he had kept his oath like an angel, and that on no consideration could he be induced to partake of the flowing bowl. "No," he would say with a decided shake of his head, "I have sworn off. If I touch it again I know I shall be a lost man. I promised my mate, George, don't you see, and when I tell you that he saved the missis and the little 'un, you'll understand that I mean to keep my word." And even while his listeners laughed they admired him, for they knew he was a better man than the best among them.

George smiled as he heard that honest snore, for he felt exceedingly proud in having thus reclaimed one of the most abandoned; for though he was no saint himself, he was not one who allowed a vice to gain the upper hand. As he watched the sleeping form of his companion he felt a paternal thrill shoot through him. Some good had come out of things evil after all.

The blessing had come in the guise of a curse, for what was the loss of the gold-dust in comparison with the well-being of this man? Phil was now one of the steadiest and tidiest members of this miscellaneous community, and though he was often the sport of the godless diggers, who mockingly called him the Reclaimed One, and the Brand plucked from the Burning, he yet had courage enough to tell them that he was reclaimed, that he had been plucked from the burning, and that he was d——d glad of it.

Vincent lit his candle, flung aside his coat and vest and undid his waist-belt, determining to have a good go at the puzzle before he turned in. To his horror, however, he could find no trace of it, and the knowledge that it was lost rushed in upon him like a frightful shock. The belt dropped from his hands and he uttered a great groan, while from out of the gloom in the far corner of the tent he thought he saw two great grey eyes fixed reproachfully on his own. Quickly picking up the belt, for hope is always with us, he once more went carefully through its several pouches, but to no purpose. There was no sign, no trace, no scrap of the precious document. What could it mean? He sprang to his feet and immediately searched his coat and vest, though he remembered well where he had last put the cipher. The search was a vain one, but he was not disappointed at its futility. Sitting down he tried hard to think what he could have done with it, or how he could by any chance have lost it. Then like a sudden inspiration came the thought that he had been drugged—drugged and robbed. He rose to his feet with a mighty oath, which made the man Phil start, as though he had been shot, and utter a truly terrifying snore. But he did not wake. He might have been sleeping off a week's drunk, so far had he gone into the land of dreams.

Drugged, robbed! Vincent paced the narrow limits of his tent like one demented, then passed out into the night and continued his mad peregrinations before the entrance of that humble dwelling. Ruined, ruined! And he thought of the sweet girl over yonder in the town, whom he had bound to him by the most extravagant oaths. Procrastinator, madman, fool! He could find no epithet strong enough to condemn his folly; nor no phrase fierce enough to hurl against those who had wrought his downfall. Had Kitty then wilfully drugged him? Could she have been guilty of a crime so heinous? He could not, he would not believe it. He knew her fierce, passionate nature, but he had, notwithstanding a few mortal errors, always looked upon her as a proud woman, and pride could never stoop to practices so degrading. Besides, what object could she have had, being ignorant of his secret? That her husband had taken her into his confidence the young man never dreamt, knowing how little they loved each other. Again, what could the husband's confidence be more than a suspicion, a thing so slight that the most daring might well stand and consider before he ventured to put it to the test? No, the thought was as degrading as it was ridiculous, and he begged her pardon over and over again.

But for her husband he had a totally different feeling. He believed in his heart of hearts that that gentleman was one in whom the god of rogues had implanted the seeds of innumerable vices, and that they had flourished and borne much fruit in days that were, and would continue to flourish till time's sweeping axe was laid to the parent root. Logan, in his opinion, was one of those creatures who will stop at nothing, and the thought that he had been robbed by that individual was one which he was perfectly willing to receive. How he had thus fallen asleep he had yet to discover; though he doubted not but that this outrage and the robbery at the camp, were planned by one and the same head. For a long time now he had entertained grave suspicions of the characters of Messrs. Logan and Smith, and he felt quite convinced that that eminent firm knew more of Ben Hall and Billy Jackson than was universally suspected. He called back to mind the night he told of the murder in Little Lonsdale Street; he recollected Logan's eagerness and fierce denunciation of Hall, and these, with his personal knowledge of the man's character, whispered a terrible secret. If Logan was the man he imagined him to be, the scoundrel Flash Jim was in close proximity to the gallows.

There was, however, one thought which gave him hope. If the cipher had defied him so long, the chances were that it would puzzle Logan longer, and in the meantime he must prepare some scheme by which he might regain possession of it. A little while ago he had congratulated himself on not having made a copy of those mystic letters; now he was as eager to censure himself for his carelessness. He might have learnt the letters, truly, but he was not certain that he had ever thought of such a thing, for hitherto the secret had seemed neither dangerous nor interesting. What he should do, or how set to work to retrieve his loss, he could not think; but he determined to make the best of a bad bargain, watch and wait, and if no other way presented itself call on the magic name of police—a word which, unless he was greatly mistaken, would have a dread significance for Messrs. Logan and Smith. And so he re-entered his primitive domicile, fastened the door-flap and turned in; but for hour after hour he lay listening to the melodious snoring of his mate Phil, constructing imaginary surprises for the obese Logan, and contemplating with pleasure and pain two great grey eyes.

But if this unhappy incident had thrown George Vincent into a fit of helpless, hopeless consternation, it would be a Herculean task to attempt to describe Kitty's feelings when she regained consciousness in the darkened room. For a long time she lay stupefied, staring up into the darkness and seeing nothing. Where she was, or how she had come there, she could not imagine, but knowing that she was not in her own bed she lay quietly, trying hard to understand the why and the wherefore of the thing. Her body ached, her brain throbbed painfully, and on pressing her hand to her mouth her lips shot sharp pains all through her.

This was the real awakening. A few quivering heart-beats, a sudden flow of burning blood to her brain, and she remembered all. With a sigh she arose to her feet, knocking her head against the table as she did so, and, with a dumb, desperate pain at her heart, groped her way to her own room.

All through the rest of that horrible night she lay in a bed of agony. Now was it for her crime she writhed, now with rage and shame; but all through, ever uppermost, glared the awful fact that she had betrayed and robbed the man she loved before all things in earth or heaven, and that henceforth a pit had been sunk between them which neither he nor she should ever over-leap. A thousand times she told herself that she had never meant to wrong him, that hope alone had urged her to the deed; but, alas! this vain assertion brought little consolation, for now that her passion was grown more calm, and her hot pride humiliated, she saw too clearly how grievous her sin had been.

Of her thoughts of Logan it would, perhaps, be profitless to speak, for they were of a nature which showed her least angelic side; but when the day began to stream in through the crevices of the blinds, she sprang from her bed, and rushing over to the little mirror carried it to the window and surveyed her face with a look of horrible calmness. There was a dark circle beneath her right eye, a great lump having arisen just by the extremity of the eyebrow, while her beautiful mouth was cut and swollen to twice its usual size. With a hard laugh, metallic in its lack of humanity, she replaced the mirror on the little dressing-table and returned to her bed. But there was a light in those injured eyes which Mr. Logan would hardly have cared to see, a determination about that injured mouth which made it hard and ugly, if such a mouth could look ugly under the most disadvantageous of circumstances.

All that day she kept her bed in spite of the threats of her husband, who now assumed conscious airs of importance, and the cajolings of Edith. She was not well, she said, and she did not think that she would dress herself. Was she very ill? Oh, dear no! Just a little out of sorts. She had, during the night, dreamt a dreadful dream, and it had so frightened her that she had thrown herself out of the bed. Hurt? Well, a little, a slight disfigurement —she was afraid she could not show up under the circumstances. Would she (Edith) mind taking her place in the bar? It should be the last time she would ask her. And the girl said yes, and expressed her sorrow with words of such loving sympathy that the guilty Kitty writhed in her loneliness, and could not hate her, though she knew that she had come between her and her soul's desire.

But as the day wore on, this wretched woman's thoughts underwent a gradual change. She had wronged Vincent beyond any hope of atonement—at least, so she had thought. But now a new idea came like a cry from heaven. There is only one crime for which no reparation can be made on earth—the crime of murder. No penance, no prayers, no tears can restore the breath into the body of the dead. We have driven it forth and it has passed beyond us into the hands of fate. The deed is done, as we have said, and not being gods it is impossible that we should mend it. But for any other sin the law of fate is not so inexorable, and we may, by penance, catch the gleam of hope. And penance is penance, though we use the word in its unclerical sense, and it has nothing whatever to do with paternosters and flagellations.

That she had most cruelly wronged this man Vincent was made so evident to her in her calmer moments that she, always more impulsive than one of her sex should be, at once determined to work out her redemption, obliterate the wrong by an act of right. He would hate her, spurn her, she doubted not, and that in itself were worse than death; but she would go to him nevertheless and say, "See, it is I who wronged you. I have come to right that wrong—forgive and let me go." And she would go from him and hide herself where no one should know her more.

Filled with this burning idea she arose as the evening drew in, and, concealing the injuries to her face very successfully by the artistic use of the contents of her toilette boxes, she descended into the bar.

"Ah, you have come," said Edith, upon beholding her. "I am so glad. Are you better, dear?"

"Yes, oh, indeed yes. But you look tired, child?"

"I have been here all day. I feel a little faint."

"Where is Mr. Logan?"

"He and Mr. Smith are in the private parlour. They have been there since the morning."

"Drinking?"

"Yes, and writing."

"Writing?"

"They have pens, ink and paper there, and I saw several sheets covered with strange groups of letters."

"So," muttered Kitty beneath her breath. Then she asked somewhat eagerly, "Have they drunk much?"

"Yes. I think they are not quite sober."

"So much the better," was the reply, but whether Mrs. Kitty spoke to herself, or addressed her cousin, it would be difficult to say. "There, there, child," she added, "run off to your room. You shall have no more work to-night. If George calls I will tell him you have had a hard day, and are very tired."

"He will not call."

"Oh! You have heard from him?" The tone was slightly suspicious.

"Yes." But as the girl seemed in no confidential mood, Kitty refrained from any exhibition of curiosity. Indeed, it was a relief to know that he had no intention of coming, for she would not have cared to look into his face just then.

Edith crept off to her room, her face paler than usual, her spirits extremely depressed. That all was not right in this house she guessed intuitively, though the nature of the wrong she could not comprehend. That it would be murder, fire, or flood she may have had her doubts, but that it would prove equally destructive she firmly believed. Therefore she double-locked her door, and for further security stood her trunk up against it, and we shall be disclosing no secrets for which our honour may upbraid us when we say that a little sigh escaped her as she thought of a pair of strong, protecting arms.

Kitty, in the meantime, stalked moodily up and down the bar like a sullen lioness in her cage, her thoughts alternately reverting to the ignominious proceedings of the previous night, and to the council of war now being held by the reputable Logan, and the no less reputable Smith. Of what they thought, and spoke, and wrote, she guessed easily enough, and trembled lest they should read the cipher before she could put her plan into execution; but trusting to the natural dulness of her spouse—for he was only smart in that smart vulgarity, that wickedness which requires no brains—she strove hard to still the tumult in her breast, and with a grimness which was almost heroic bided her time.

Presently the bell of the private parlour rang, and, putting on a repentant and humble look, she hastened to obey the summons. Arriving at the door, she knocked gently and attempted to open it at the same time, but to her surprise found it locked.

"Never mind the door," shouted Logan from within, "fetch us some more whisky, and look sharp about it."

Kitty turned away with a scowl on her face, not having spoken a word. A few moments later she returned with two stiff glasses of whisky, and knocked again.

"What is it?" shouted her husband.

"Whisky."

"Oh!"

She heard little bursts of partly-smothered laughter, and a few words of hurried conversation. Then the door was opened by the worthy landlord, who greeted her with a broad grin.

"You, Kit," he said. "I thought it was the girl."

"She has gone to bed tired out." Unheeding the grinning and impertinent stare of both her husband and the man Smith, she walked quietly over to the table and deposited the whisky thereon.

"What's this?" cried Logan, holding up one of the glasses.

"Whisky," she answered.

"How do I know it is?" he asked with an exasperating grin.

"Drink it and you will see."

"No, thank you, Mrs. L. I have no particular wish to go to sleep at the present moment; because, you see, it isn't safe where women are. You take this back, my dear, and bring me an unopened bottle."

Without a word she took up the liquor

and departed, though her pulse throbbed many a beat quicker, and the blood rushed up to her brain and turned her giddy. As she made her way back to the bar she heard the coarse laughter of the two men, but she only put her teeth together. The play was not finished yet.

"That's something like a wife," cried Logan admiringly, as she re-entered the room with an unopened bottle of whisky in her hand, " that's what I call a dutiful spouse. What do you say, Sammy?"

Mr. Smith grinned stupidly, being the worse for drink, but made no reply.

"You think it was about time I took her in hand, eh, old pal?" continued Mr. Logan with a drunken leer at his boon companion. "Well, you know," he went on sententiously, " a woman's all the better for a little wholesome consideration. Being a creature of impulse, she must learn the virtue of restraint. They are like unbroken fillies,

Sammy, they love to run wild; and yet I've heard it said they like to feel the curb, too, because they are wise enough to know that it's for their own good."

"The curb is good, Peter, even though it cuts the mouth."

Logan laughed loudly at this coarse allusion to his wife's swollen lips, and Mr. Smith hissed in his own peculiar way. Kitty turned hot and cold, and might have done some damage there and then had she the wherewithal; but controlling her anger with a great effort, she asked meekly if they had any further orders to give.

"There," exclaimed Logan, proudly, "what do you think of that? Isn't that a wife for you, isn't that an obedient, civil wife? I tell you what it is, Sammy, there's nothing a woman respects so much as a good licking."

"Nor a man either," replied the sapient

Smith. "That's the thing to make them mind their p's and q's."

"Shall you want me any more?" asked Kitty, edging towards the door.

"No, my darling," hiccuped Mr. Logan. "Only be a good girl, Kit, always be a good girl, or I shall have to spank you again, and remember, I have a good deal to pay off yet." She bowed her head, and without a word departed, while he, turning to his companion with a smile of triumph, said, "I guess that licking has been the making of her, Sammy, old pal."

"That's as may be," replied the ambiguous Samuel. "But I don't trust 'em, Peter, and less than ever when they come the sucking-dove business. They're bad, Peter, take 'em in a lump, and I never trusted a petticoat yet that I wasn't sorry for it."

Logan laughed. "I've scotched that devil anyway."

"When devils are only scotched they grow strong again," suggested the wily Smith. "But let us get on with this infernal puzzle. How old Ben could have taken the trouble to make up a fool of a thing like this gets over me. No wonder old Billy carried it about so long. He wouldn't have made it out in a hundred years."

"We don't seem to be getting very near the solution ourselves," suggested the worthy Boniface.

"That's true," remarked his companion, "but we've got the paper, Peter, and if we hadn't muddled our heads with so much drink we'd have found out the answer long ago."

"We'll swear off after to-day."

"Till we've read the puzzle," added Mr. Smith quickly.

"Pre—cisely," said Logan with a grin.

Then they replenished their glasses—by

way of sealing their good resolutions — toasted each other on the fortune which had so suddenly fallen into their hands, lit two strong cigars—to help to clear their heads—then sat down, asking each other what that old fool Ben could have meant by drawing up such a fool of a puzzle.

CHAPTER V.

THE REDEMPTION OF KITTY.

AND while all this was going on in the private parlour, Mrs. Kitty presided over her beer-taps with a silence and dignity quite depressing. Not a single smile broke over her solemn, sphinx-like face during the whole of that evening. She might have been a marble woman for all the life there seemed in her. Never had the habitués of the "Emu's Head" seen their patron saint in such a cheerless mood, and though they crowded round the pewter-laden shrine as usual, and asked numerous sympathetic questions as to the contusion on her face and the swollen lips, she could find no word of comfort for them, not even a little smile. She had met with an accident, was all that she would say—a statement readily credited, for no one dreamt that Logan would have dared to touch her. Had some of her more ardent devotees known the facts of the case, they would have given that gentleman something to remember till the day of his death.

But at last the long hours came to an end, the house was cleared, the lights extinguished, and the inhabitants supposed to be in bed ; and so they all were with the exception of Mrs. Kitty, Messrs. Logan and Smith. Those worthy men still sat over their whisky, wondering what that old fool Ben could have meant by drawing up such a fool of a puzzle ; while Mrs. Kitty stood trembling in her doorway wondering if they would ever go to bed that night, and if the quantity of alcohol they had taken would prove sufficient to enable her to carry out her design.

At last the door of the little room was opened, and by the light which streamed into the dark passage, she saw the man Smith stagger forth.

"I'm going to bed," he shouted. "If you prefer a chair, you're welcome to it, Jimmy, old pal."

"Jimmy!" She wondered if the word had really escaped her. To her it seemed as though she had shouted it at the top of her voice. Pressing her hand to her heart she strained her ears to listen.

"Ugh!" grunted the man, "the fat pig's asleep already," and as if in confirmation of this statement a resonant snore came buzzing along the passage. Mr. Smith emitted a low chuckle as he staggered off to his room, and presently the trembling listener heard him slam his door as if he intended to bring the house down.

Five, six, ten minutes she waited, her heart throbbing so loudly that it seemed to ring like the brazen voice of a bell. A century of doubt and fear she experienced in those few moments. And still she moved not, listening—listening, as though she expected something to happen. But beyond the numerous strange sounds which one hears of a night, which come from and go no-whither, and the occasional buzzing snore from the room below, there was nothing of which a determined and desperate woman might be afraid. With one hand pressed firmly on her heart, and a tightening of the lips which must let no sound escape them, she descended the half-dozen steps which led to the passage. Gliding softly along the thick oilcloth, for she was in her stockinged feet, she quickly reached the door of the little room, though she hung back for a moment in the darkness, counting her husband's regular breathings. Her heart now began to beat faster and louder than ever, and a violent trembling assailed her, which at one time threatened destruction to her enterprise; but she pressed her two hands on her breast as though she would choke back the blood that set her in a whirl, bit her swollen lips till they bled afresh, and, with a determination born of despair, stepped into the doorway.

The lamp still burnt brightly, so that she was enabled to take in every feature of the room at a glance. Therefore her consternation was extreme when she beheld her husband sitting facing her, his eyes wide open. An exclamation rose to her lips, for she thought he saw her, but with a mighty effort she stifled it, remembering that he often slept with his eyes open. Yet it was no easy nor pleasant thing to stand there, look into those hideous eyes, and yet not speak. It was a full minute before she recovered the use of her faculties, and not till she had listened to his regular breathings, and marked the rise and fall of his expansive chest, could she quite believe that he was unconscious of her presence.

With a noiseless movement she glided into the room, her eyes wandering from his face to the table, which was littered with papers. With a rapid eye she scanned these papers for that frayed and yellow piece which she had sunk so low to gain, but to her disappointment she saw nothing but a few irregular letters here and there, plainly showing that the confederates had not gone to work with much method or zest. Yet she was not one who would allow herself to be thus easily beaten, and with a desperate look on her face, she stepped up to her husband's chair and stared fiercely into his senseless eyes. No answering look broke from them, however. She might have been gazing into the glassy eyes of the dead. Indeed there was something supernatural about such a sight, and she shuddered in spite of her hate and determination.

But there was yet work to do, and with eyes glued fiercely to his, and lips closed hard so that no breath might betray her, she leant over him, and into his breast-pocket inserted her long, flexible fingers, extracting a piece of paper therefrom. This, however, not proving to be that for which she searched, again her fingers dipped into the recess, and this time she drew forth an old envelope. Opening it with fingers which shook in spite of her resolution, she beheld the little yellow slip lying snugly within. Her heart gave a great throb, almost forcing from her a sharp cry, and, lest her joy should be the means of her undoing, she made immediately for the door. Half way across the room, however, she was startled by hearing her husband cry, "Ah!" and, looking over her shoulder, stood petrified with fear, for he had partly risen from his chair; his eyes glared fiercely and his huge fist was raised as though in the act of striking. Thinking that she was discovered she was about to turn defiantly on him, when he sank back in his chair once more, the fist dropped helplessly to his side and he began to mutter vaguely. It was evident that Mr. Logan was not accustomed to undisturbed repose.

In a moment Kitty had quitted the apartment, and, stooping down to pick up her shoes, which she had deposited outside the room, she groped her way through the dark passage till she reached the street-door. Opening this as stealthily as any burglar, she passed out into the night. For a good two hundred yards she hurried on in her stockinged feet, then, sitting on a door-step, she swiftly slipped on her shoes and rushed off again in the direction of the camp.

It was with an exultant cry that she

entered the open country. The night was dark, but there were many stars above, and somehow the darkness seemed a long way off. There was a beating at her breast, a throbbing in her brain, which gave her kinship with those celestial bodies, and she rushed on through the night as they through space — an immortal. She was about to make reparation, sue for forgiveness, right a great wrong, fill with joy the heart of him she loved, though it would break her own. And even amid her shame, and all the unknown horror of the future, she felt proud, and glad, and happy. Never till this hour had she known how grand it is to right a wrong, how sweet and heroic it is to feel truly humble. The thought of this restoration and of her supplication caused her more joy than had her fiercest, most passionate dreams of love. They would part for ever, she knew that, he to go his way, she hers; but even that thought left a less disagreeable flavour than her guilty dreams. There is a wondrous sweetness in martyrdom, despite the scoffing of the cynics, and in her present state of excitement this reparation sprang up like the flame of a religious enthusiasm. Nor sword nor stake would have made her falter now. Her purpose was fixed; immutable as the stars above her. Poor Kitty, thou shouldst have seen other times and other ways.

In the meantime, Mr. George Vincent, little dreaming of the change which was now so imminent, for he had not seen those shadows which the poet tells us precede events, tossed restlessly in his bunk. For hour after hour he had turned and twisted on his wretched mattress, a prey to the most conflicting emotions; but, try as he would, he could not coax the sweet soother to his side. Then he lit his pipe and smoked long and steadily; then he tried to construct the letters in proper order, but the worst of that attempt was that he would never know when he had constructed them properly. Then he tried to think of Edith (though that required little trying), and of making his fortune without the aid of chance, though he liked not the idea over well. She, dear girl, would come to him when and how he pleased; but, loving her as he did, he could not drag her down to his own wretched level. That he would see the cipher again he scarcely hoped, for guessing who had it, and knowing well what it meant to such men, he looked upon his chances as extremely remote, though he had determined not yet to yield the day. Logan should be well watched: if he attempted to leave the place, Vincent was determined to set the police upon him. And if, in the meantime, the secret of the writing was discovered, he would take good care that they did not remove the treasure without molestation. For the rest, he must remain quiet; though he had some notion of accusing Logan to his face, and threatening him with the police, believing that such a threat would mean more than it usually does.

And as he lay constructing and re-constructing his imaginary lines of action, while his mate, Phil, snored away as complacently as though there were no such thing as trouble in the world, and the wind sighed mournfully round the corners of the tent, he was suddenly awakened to other thoughts than these by hearing a soft foot-fall outside. It stopped at the side of the tent, or close against his head, then slowly made its way to the entrance. Now he heard the hands going over the canvas searching for the flap, or door; and raising himself gently on one arm he drew his revolver from beneath his pillow and prepared himself to shoot, for that the intruder could be there with an honest purpose he never imagined. Presently he heard a scratching on the canvas; then one of the buckles was unfastened and an aperture made in the flap, and he beheld the outline of a face fill in the hole. Slowly, carefully he raised his revolver, and in another moment the intruder might have paid dearly for such rashness.

" George !"

The whisper came only in time. At that word the revolver fell to his side.

" Kitty?"

" Yes—I want you."

" In a moment." Vincent was out of bed and had slipped on his clothes ere one could count a hundred. What could she want? Of course, it could only be to tell him one thing. Some calamity had befallen Edith!

He stepped out into the night and saw her standing by the far corner of the tent.

"What is it?" he asked excitedly. "Has anything happened to her?"

"No—not that I know of."

"Then—then what in heaven's name brings you out here at such a time?"

"I have come to ask you a favour."

"Ask me?" he stammered. "I—I don't quite understand."

This, indeed, was getting serious. It is one thing to know that a woman is fond of you, but it is another to have that woman ever at your heels. Vincent, being a modest youth, grew somewhat flurried as he thought, and was both shocked and grieved to think that women could really do such things.

Kitty, however, gave him little time for further speculation. Throwing herself on her knees before him, she, bowing her head, said, "I have come to ask your forgiveness."

"My forgiveness?" he cried. "But come, you must not kneel to me. You could do nothing which should need so humble a repentance."

"I have done that," she sobbed, "for which I scarcely dare hope for pardon; and as for repentance, if that would only blot out my shame, I would kneel for ever."

A sudden thought struck him as he helped her to her feet.

"Kitty," he exclaimed, pressing her hands excitedly, "it was not you—it was not you who——" He could not say the word, but she said it for him.

"Yes—it was I who robbed you."

"Good God!"

"Hear me, George, and know me for what I am. I deliberately planned the outrage; drugged you, robbed you. What do you think of me?"

"Oh!" he cried, stepping back as though her presence were pollution, "it's horrible, horrible! And I had always thought you the grandest woman in the world."

There was something in this last sentence which smote her aching heart, driving the bitter tears to her eyes. The grandest woman in the world! Only think of it! To be thus, even in the eyes of one man, is a position few women attain. What a friend was here if she had only known, if she had only known!

"My bitterest regret is the forfeiture of your respect. Forgive me, oh, forgive me!"

"With all my heart," he said.

"God bless you, George!"

For a moment there was silence between them, her sobs alone keeping time with the wailing of the wind. Presently he spoke.

"Tell me," he said, "what induced you

to treat me so—you whom I loved so much? What had I ever done to you that you should have sought for this revenge?"

"Nothing, nothing. It was the evil which was in me, the jealousy, the despair. I wanted to prevent your marriage."

"Why?"

"Why!" she echoed, with an hysterical moan, a heart-broken moan—a cry that went to the heart—"Why! Oh, my God! because I loved you better than my own soul."

"Hush!" he cried, " you must not say that. You don't know what it means."

"Yes—yes; but I wanted you to know. Perhaps you will understand now why I did what I have done?"

"I am sorry for you," he answered sadly, " but I shall never understand your motive. Neither she nor I had ever injured you in any way."

"Never injured me!" she began, almost

fiercely; then, stopping suddenly, answered gently, "No, no—of course not. It is I who have been mistaken all through, I who have been all to blame. Yet, believe me, I never meant that others should profit by your loss."

"I would rather have spent my days in want than that you should have done this thing. God help you, Kitty, and forgive you as freely as I do."

Kitty sobbed aloud as though her heart had broken.

"You will let the girl stay on a little, won't you?" he asked. "I may strike gold at any moment, and then I will repay you for all your goodness."

"Goodness! You are mocking me. But if I could sin, George, don't think that I am wholly abandoned. I have had no peace of mind ever since that dreadful business. To-night I came not only to beg your forgiveness, but to atone for the past. Listen to me, George. I robbed you because I loved you; I now return what I stole because I love you still. Here is the paper—the cipher. Take it, and God be with you!" She pressed the cause of all their woe into his hand and turned to depart.

"Stay," he cried. "What is this you have done?"

She told him all, even how her brutal husband had felled her to the ground.

"The marks are on me now," she said, "but they no longer sting."

"Did he dare?" exclaimed the young fellow, involuntarily clenching his fist.

"I thought I should have killed him," she continued, unheeding the question; "but when I remembered your wrong, I knew I could bear my own."

"But he is a desperate man. If he finds out that you have brought this to me——"

"He would kill me. Yes, I know it; but I don't mind now."

There was a tone of such utter melancholy in her voice that Vincent hesitated to break the silence.

"I suppose you have often wondered," she said, as if reading his thoughts, "why I ever came to marry such a man. I often wonder myself, and think I must have been mad at the time. I know I hated home, for ours was a wretched life. I had no friends. Those for whom I cared at school were not allowed to associate with me after. And, when mother died, father took to drink, and sank, sank, till I was ashamed to go out in the streets, for people nudged each other as they looked at me, and I knew of what they were speaking. Then *he* came, and he seemed good enough in his own coarse way. But I had no love for him—never a grain. He released me from prison, and I was thankful."

"Poor Mrs Kitty. I am sorry, so sorry."

"Don't, don't," she moaned, "I cannot bear it. I have wrecked my life, and I know there is nothing for me this side of the grave. With other chances I might have been different, but I was beaten at the start."

Vincent was greatly distressed at the passionate ring of anguish in her tones, but what could he do? The merest human kindness, under such conditions, might transform itself into that which could but deepen the wound; for Pain and Suffering are the twin brothers of Hope and Joy, and in the bosom of one is born the life of the other.

"And now what shall you do?" he asked at length.

"I must go back. I will take care of Edith till you come for her. Then I will go away."

"Away—where?"

"I don't know. The world is wide, and it doesn't matter much where I pull up at last."

"You must not talk like this; you shall not. If I find this treasure your fortune shall be my care."

"Ah!" she cried, with a strange, pathetic outburst, "how was it possible for me to understand a man like you? I would give twenty years of my life never to have injured you."

"You have not injured me. It was a momentary wrong, that is all, which* is over now, forgiven and forgotten. Without it I should never have known one-half of your nobility."

"Nobility!" she echoed.

"Ay, nobility, heroism, grandeur. What you have done to-night has stamped you as one of the bravest of God's brave creatures. It was an action needing more courage than men are called upon to show on the deadliest battle-field. We are friends, we must be friends."

"Yes, yes."

"And now we must think of the morrow. First of all, let me accompany you back to the town, and as we walk we will arrange our plans for the future. We are allies now, you know, and must present a threatening front to the common enemy."

"My husband?"

"Well, yes. Why should I seek to deny what I know to be true?"

"There is no reason. Good-night."

"You will let me go with you?"

"No, no!"

"Why not?"

"Cannot you understand," she cried, her voice full of the bitterest anguish, "that it will be better for me to go alone?"

"I beg your pardon."

"After to-night," she said in a tremulous voice, "we must blot out the entire past—

forget that there has ever been aught between us which might make us regret that we had ever known each other. You may trust me now. I will guard Edith with my life; it shall be a part of my penance; and when the time comes for you to take her away, you shall say to me, 'Well done'; and it shall be counted in my favour at the end."

Sob after sob shook her frame, and the great tears glistened like diamonds as they chased each other down her cheeks.

"Don't cry, Mrs. Kitty," he said, feeling a great lump rising in his own throat, "don't, there's a good girl. I know you are a brave, true woman at heart, and now you see your way I am sure you will try hard to follow it."

"Yes, yes—trust me, only trust me."

"With my life," he said.

There was a pause for a moment or two, and it was evident to him, as he watched the tumultuous rising and falling of her breast, that she was grappling with some sudden and exciting thought. Twice she turned from him as if to go, but each time swung round again and faced him. Her eyes shone like two great stars, and through her lips came the breath in little gasps.

With a quick movement she took his two hands in hers. "I feel," she said, "that this parting will be entirely different from what we imagine. The thought, the presentiment—call it what you will—came to me just as I turned to go. It seemed as though a voice whispered in my ear, 'To-morrow! Who knows where we may be, or what shall have befallen us?'"

"A fancy," he said, though he felt partly awed by the melancholy of her tone.

"No doubt. And yet—and yet! George," she cried almost imploringly, "will you, will you kiss me once more—just once more?" He drew back hesitant. "It will not be wronging her, and for us to-morrow may never dawn."

He stooped and kissed her on the forehead as a father might his daughter.

"No, no," she cried, "on the lips, on the lips."

And he kissed her full on her hot and swollen mouth, and for a moment her brain whirled giddily, like one who is about to faint; then with a cry, half-sob, half-moan, she bounded from his side and disappeared into the night.

CHAPTER VI.

DELILAH PAYS.

Mr. Peter Logan slept on in his easy armchair, his eyes wide open, his lips muttering vague words and phrases. Ever and anon great gasps rose from his massive throat, and his hands opened and shut convulsively. It was painfully evident that serenity was not the presiding genius of his slumber. Indeed, at the moment in which we revisit the little sitting-room, he was undergoing a fearful, though fanciful, experience. He dreamt that old Billy Jackson had come to him, his throat dripping blood, his clothes mud-bespattered and sodden with rain: had robbed him of the cipher and made off with the bags of gold slung over his shoulders, singing, the meanwhile, in a mocking voice which seemed to come from the gash in his throat, that exquisite stanza which had consigned the late lamented Mr. Benjamin Hall to the abode of the wicked. For a moment the dreamer stood choking with rage and terror, unable to move, glued to the spot by some invisible means. Then, of a sudden, the unseen manacles fell from his limbs and he darted after the mocking songster; but when he clutched those bags they melted like gossamer in his hands, and from the rent he made a torrent of blood spouted into his face, and all the while the hideous spectre chanted his horrible song. Wiping the blood from his eyes the dreamer rushed furiously upon the dreadful thing, when, lo and behold, in its place stood his wife, decked out in the white robes of the dead, a great gash in her throat from which the red blood gushed. Blood, blood! The world was full of blood. With a horrible shriek he awoke, trembling in every limb, the sweat starting from every pore in his body. Luckily the light had not yet burnt out, so that he was quickly re-assured as to the unsubstantiality of his vision. Sobered he was, too, or at least sufficiently sensible to know that the best thing he could do would be to get between the sheets as soon as possible.

It was a terrible dream, though, and as he arose, quivering to his heart's core, he beheld the scattered papers on the table and instinctively dipped into his pocket for the cipher. Discovering it not, he stared about him like one amazed; then went rapidly through his pockets, but fruitlessly. He next proceeded to search amid the papers on the table, but with a like result.

"I've been robbed," he cried with a terrible oath, "robbed!"

And if there was any man alive at that

moment who felt an utter abhorrence of all dishonesty, it was Mr. Peter Logan.

With a hurried, though elephantine tread, he paced the little room, trying hard to think, for thinking came not easy to this worthy man even in his most idyllic periods, therefore we must not expect too much from him to-night; but the more he thought the more certain was he that Mr. Samuel Smith had plundered him, for his own ends. This raised his evil Irish blood to boiling pitch, and vowing death and destruction, if his surmises should prove correct, he made at once for the room of his perfidious associate. Rob a pal would he, the dog; a pal who had stood by him through thick and thin? He gasped, he trembled with rage. Such black ingratitude seemed to him the crown of baseness, and he was shocked beyond measure at man's awful depravity.

With a wonderfully quiet step he

approached his victim's door and turned the handle softly, as though he had been used to such things. All was quiet, save for the melodious breathings of the estimable Smith, and Logan, knowing the lay of the room so well, advanced to the bed with a quick, noiseless step, and seized his boon companion by the throat.

With a dreadful scream the sleeping man awoke, but feeling the fierce grip on his throat, and being naturally confused by such a terrible awakening, he did little more than scream, thinking the devil had got him fast.

"Hand it over," hissed the devil, "hand it over, I tell you, or I won't leave a breath in your cursed body."

This was truly no devil's voice, or at least the voice of no supernatural devil, and Mr. Smith began to struggle desperately.

"Let me go," he gasped, "let me go, you fool."

"I'll shake the life out of you first," hissed the fool, and the great fingers pressed tighter round the throat.

"Jim—Jim—for God's sake, old pal!"

But the word "pal" only added a fiercer resolve to those terrible fingers. They seemed to stiffen and grow sharp, pressing the throat's apple right up into the mouth. Smith thought his time had come, knowing the nature of his assailant, and in a half-dazed, yet wholly furious state, he hit upwards with his clenched fist. In a moment the hands about his throat relaxed their awful grip, and his would-be murderer fell to the floor with a loud groan.

Hurriedly springing from his bed, upon which he had been lying in his clothes, Mr. Smith lit a candle and discovered Logan sitting on the floor, rolling from side to side in agony, his two hands pressed to the pit of his stomach; for upon that extensive portion of his person had the worthy Smith's fist uprisen with wonderful effect.

"Oh, you cur," moaned Logan as soon as he could find wind enough to sound his thought, "you cur, to hit a man below the belt." This, at least, was the simple meaning of his words, though the expletives he indulged in would have made a bullock-driver sick with envy.

There was something entertaining in this man's protest, at any rate there appeared so to his companion—for, in spite of his terror, Smith could not conceal the smile which played about his pale lips.

"You're a nice one, you are, to talk about hitting a man below the belt. Why, you'd have murdered me in another minute."

"That's right," said Logan, wagging his big head, "I would. I'd have done it, Sammy, if you hadn't hit me that coward's blow."

"Coward's blow," repeated Smith with an ugly grin. "Well, that's as may be, but I thank my stars I'm not your sort of cur, old pal."

"Then hand over the paper," said Logan, still pressing his stomach as though it pained him sorely. "The man who robs a pal is no mate for me."

Again the wintry smile played round Smith's pale lips.

"What's the game, Peter?" The question was asked quietly enough, but there was a world of meaning in the man's tone, the effect of which was not lost upon the worthy landlord.

"Game," he growled, "I've lost Ben's cipher, that's the game, and you've got it."

"Oh, indeed," sneered Smith.

"Yes, 'oh indeed,'" fumed Logan; "and it will be a bad game too unless you hand it over."

"Come, Jimmy—I mean Peter," said Mr.

Smith, accentuating the name, "this sort of thing won't do."

"What do you mean?" asked Logan, rising to his feet with an effort.

"I mean that I am going to have half of Ben's Plant—or know the reason why," he added with a truly diabolical look.

"Oh," said Logan with a grin, "you don't believe I've lost it, eh?"

"I do not. And what's more, old pal, I mean to have my share, so make your mind easy on that."

"You're a fool," said Logan. "I tell you the thing's gone. I hope I may swing before I'm three months older if it's not the truth I'm telling you. It was in this pocket when I fell asleep in the chair. Now it's gone, and if you haven't taken it, who has?"

Smith began to look uneasy. There was a ring of truth in the landlord's voice which convinced him against his will.

"If I could only believe you," he said.

"It's hard that a man should be doubted when it's the gospel he's speaking," moaned Mr. Logan pathetically.

"Well, you know, Peter," said his companion, softly yet impressively, "I'd like to believe you, but then you was always such a dreadful liar."

Mr. Logan smiled. "Well," he said, "I could never give you any points at that game, old pal, for I never believed a word you ever told me."

"And yet you expect me to believe you?"

"It's the truth whether you believe it or not." And as Mr. Logan forgot to adorn this statement with strings of sacred and profane oaths, a thing he invariably did when lying, his companion felt convinced that there was some shade of truth in the story.

"Then I suppose I must believe you," he

said; "so let us get to business. Have you thought of anyone but me who might have found the paper useful?"

"No—because Vincent wasn't here. No one could have got it but you."

"Not even the missis?"

"She wouldn't dare. Besides——"

"My dear Peter, if I remember rightly, she refused to give up the paper on any consideration, and it was not till you had thumped her a bit that you succeeded in obtaining it?"

"That's so."

"Now why should she refuse to give it up?"

"Why—unless it was to benefit herself —or her lover?" he added between his teeth.

"Pre—cisely, Peter. I'm glad to see your brains isn't yet run to fat."

Mr. Logan acknowledged this compliment by no sign. Indeed, it might be doubtful whether he really heard it, so absorbed seemed he in thought.

"No," said he at last, as though speaking to himself, "she'd never dare, never dare."

"Peter, old pal, the ways of woman is pe—culiar. There's no knowing what they won't do or dare, and if I was you I'd go and pay her a visit—just t' see how's she's getting along," he added with a chuckle.

"The very thing," cried Logan excitedly, turning towards the door. "Come with me."

The two men left the room and crept quietly up the few stairs which led to Kitty's bedroom, but great was Logan's consternation when he saw the door wide open. Into the chamber he flew like a colossal fury, the estimable Smith at his heels, but no Kitty was to be found. The bed had not even been slept in that night.

"Gone!" gasped the landlord.

"So it seems."

"Wait a minute." He seized the candle and darted off.

"What is it?" cried his companion.

"She may be in with the girl."

Presently there was a knocking and a sound of voices, and a minute later Logan re-appeared.

"No—she's not there," he said.

"Then she's done it, sure enough. Let us go and have a look at the front door."

They descended into the hall, and on examining the door found that every bolt was withdrawn, and that the door itself was shut only by the ordinary catch-lock, so that anyone, by simply turning the handle, could have opened it from the outside.

"Dangerous," muttered Logan, "and so many rogues about."

"Yes, ain't it?" grinned his companion. "What do you think of it, Sammy?"

"It's plain enough, ain't it? She's cleared off with the cipher to her lover."

Logan uttered a terrible oath.

"If I knew it for certain," he said, "it would be the last time she should play any man false."

"Suppose we follow her," suggested Mr. Smith in a low tone. "She may not have had much of a start, and we may overtake her. If not, we're bound to meet her coming back."

"Curse her!" hissed Logan.

"Well," said Smith, "I never could see the use of women myself, even though they've cost me so much; though that, I reckon, was due to my own weakness. As I said before, mate, you take 'em in a lump and you'll find that lump a mighty bad bargain. No good ever came out of 'em yet, and if I had my way I'd lock 'em up like the Turks do, or bowstring 'em— which is better."

"I hope for her sake we shan't meet her," said Logan, " there will be the devil to pay if we do." And he slipped from the side of his companion, saying he was going to get a hat.

Mr. Smith grinned; thought of the whisky bottle on the table inside, and then buttoned his coat up round his neck, feeling, under the circumstances, quite glad that he had been unable to undress himself that night. Thus, even inebriation has sometimes its advantages.

In a few moments the landlord reappeared, and, carefully closing the door behind them, the two men set out in the direction of the camp.

Logan was exceedingly morose during that journey, and to the chatter of his companion replied with rude monosyllables which, under less inspiring circumstances, would have checked Mr. Smith's exuberance; for that worthy man chirped, with a persistency quite aggravating to his sullen companion, that exquisite relation of the doings of the late lamented Mr. Benjamin Hall on the plains of Avernus.

> " But fate ordained the rifle's roar
> Should prove his parting knell;
> And so he robs on earth no more,
> But bails them up in h—, h—, h—,
> But bails them up in h—"

And the way that good man emphasised the last word of this rhyme showed what a warm interest he took in his future home. Perhaps he dreamt of some joyful excursions, in company with Mr Benjamin Hall, along the " night's Plutonian shore." Who shall say ? Even the most depraved of us have our dreams. Certain it is that, like a true hero, Smith's spirits rose at the thought of fighting, especially when he knew that it was not likely to cause him any injury. That Logan meant to be revenged he doubted not, and that was delightful in itself; but what that revenge would be, what form it would take, opened up a splendid vista of boundless possibility. He, too, had an old score to settle with the haughty Kitty, for, from the moment he had crossed the threshold of the "Emu's Head," she had treated him with systematic disdain, and though his skin was thicker than a woman's, it was not so tough as an elephant's.

When they reached the rather dilapidated bridge, which spanned the creek some quarter of a mile above the camp, Mr. Smith suggested a halt, remarking that this of all places would be the one where they were most likely to meet her, a remark which seemed to coincide with the landlord's own thoughts, for he was already resting against the railings of the bridge, staring sullenly down into the black water, which, swollen by the late rains, roared angrily as it dashed among the wooden piers.

They, however, had barely taken up their position when the sound of hurrying footsteps fell upon their ears, and instinctively the two men knelt in the shadow of the beams.

"It's the missis," whispered Smith.

Logan spoke not, but his companion heard him gasping for breath, and knew that he was fearfully excited.

On Kitty came at a great pace, her head down, as though she could no longer hold her face up to the stars, and it was not till she was within half-a-dozen yards of the two men that she became aware of their presence.

She started back with a little cry, but, recognising her husband, exclaimed:

"You!"

"Yes, me. What are you doing out here?"

She noted the passion in his voice, but was not one to be cowed by a word, and so replied boldly:

"That is my business," and started forward as though she would pass.

He pushed her back with a blow on the shoulder.

"Stay where you are," he hissed, "or it will be the worse for you. Where have you been?"

"What is that to you?" she asked defiantly.

"You shall see presently," he cried hoarsely. "You have been to your lover, woman."

"It's a lie," she cried passionately "a wicked lie."

"You deny then, that you have been to Vincent?"

"No, I do not."

He laughed harshly. "I thought you wouldn't have the impudence to brazen it out. You have given him the paper you stole from me?"

"I gave him the paper which was

rightly his; I gave him the paper which you murdered Billy Jackson to get."

A fearful oath escaped Logan's lips, and it was as well night hid the ghastly look of rage on his face, for it was too terrible to behold. Smith shrank farther back against the bridge and wished himself well out of the business.

"You fool," hissed the landlord in an intensely nervous voice, "you don't know what you are saying."

"Perhaps not," she replied; "but I am not such a fool as you seem to think, *Jim Regan!*"

Logan sprang upon her with a savage cry and seized her by the arms close up to the shoulders, pressing his fingers into her soft flesh till she could have shrieked with the pain.

"Who told you that?" he cried.

"Then it is true—you are Flash Jim?"

"True or not," he said in a low voice,

which sounded like the snarling of a dog, "it would have been better for you if you had minded your own business."

"This is my business," she answered boldly enough, though her heart began to fail her; "let me go."

He laughed derisively. "I'll let you go, yes, but, by God, you shan't come back!"

His voice was brutal, terrible; a voice of passion and infernal malice. Quickly drawing her to him he seized her by the throat, and in a moment had her on the ground, his knee upon her breast. She struggled wildly, fiercely; but Smith, seizing both her hands, rendered her powerless. Then she grew still, still, till there seemed no breath nor motion in her, and the murderers rested for a moment. Then, without a word, Logan seized her under the arms, his companion taking her feet, and together they carried her to the rails of the bridge. With a one, two, three—they swung her out into the darkness. There was a splash as her body struck the black water; then all was still save for the dirge-like melody the wild stream chanted.

The two men turned from the ghostly spot and fled away into the shadows of the night.

CHAPTER VII.

THE CIPHER.

Totally unconscious of the tragedy which was being enacted within half a mile of him, George Vincent re-entered his tent, having paced before the door of that humble mansion for a good ten minutes after Kitty's departure, turning and twisting the points of her extraordinary confession. That she should have been guilty of such a crime as that to which she had confessed, filled him with horror; yet in the face of her atonement that horror almost approached the verge of admiration, for to him there seemed something grand in such a strong nature. That, liking him so well—and by her own words he was bound to believe that she did —she could have committed a crime so despicable, seemed a thing contrary to his nature; but that having sinned, having sunk so low, having so cruelly outraged her pride and debased her dignity, she yet had courage enough to face the shameful penance, confess her fault with tears of her heart's blood, with words whose shame made her poor ears burn and tingle, was to him, in spite of all her faults, proof positive of the innate nobility of her soul. It is one thing to be genuinely sorry—even the worst of us must feel compunction for our crimes—but it is another to heap the dust upon our head, array ourselves in the glaring robes of shame, and stand up for the world to see.

Entering the tent he struck a light and lit the candle, a proceeding which awakened the Brand plucked from the Burning.

"Hollo, mate," he exclaimed, "what's up?"

"I'm going to do a little work, old man."

Do you think you could sleep with this burning?"

"Bless you, yes." And as if to suit the action to the word he turned his back on Vincent and began to snore.

George laughed. "Very well," he said, "you snore as much as you like, Phil, and don't take any notice of me."

"Is it a long job, mate?"

"I'm afraid it may be."

"Can I be of any service?"

"No, thank you."

The Reclaimed One answered with a snore, and Vincent set to work.

The first thing he did was to extract some note-paper from a book, and this, with a lead pencil, he placed beside the candle on his trunk, which he had stood upon one end the better to act its part of table. Then placing a low three-legged stool beside it, he sat carefully down, for one of the legs was a bit shaky, and with much deliberation brought out from the depths of his waistcoat pocket the mystic paper. This he unfolded slowly, breathing a silent prayer for light as he did so; but those terrifying letters stared out as blankly at him as they did on that memorable night three years ago. He read and re-read the writing a score of times in twenty different ways; across, up and down, at all sorts of angles, from top to bottom and *vice versâ;* yet he could make nothing of it, nor, try as he would, could he remember how previously he had read the words, *Dead Man's Flat.* In fact, so mystified did he become, that he grew doubtful if he really had read them, for he recollected well that he caught them in a glimpse, as it were, and that they had vanished as swiftly and mysteriously as they had come. Then he began to jot down the letters at odd intervals till he had both sides of one sheet of paper covered with figures. Yet he seemed no nearer the secret, for though he found himself constructing words with comparative ease, the letters which formed them were annexed so arbitrarily that they led to ultimate confusion.

The seconds ran into minutes, the minutes hours, and yet he plodded doggedly on, though it was with a feeling of despair. He grew to hate the sight of the paper; the cursed letters danced before him like so many will-o'-the wisps, and, had it not been for the sake of another, it is ten to one he would have torn that vexatious writing into a thousand pieces. His candle burnt low and spluttered; he arose and lit another, hoping the change would bring him luck, but instead of that it only annoyed him more, for it burnt vilely. At length he arose in despair, and lighting his pipe at that provoking stick of tallow, which he succeeded in doing after partly extinguishing it with an avalanche of ash, he stepped outside into the night and began to pace restlessly up and down.

It was no good, so ran his thoughts; he would never be able to discover the secret. Curse it! He hadn't the brains of a kangaroo. Poor Edith. He was afraid she would have to rest contented with a humble hut, or fly at higher game. One thing was certain—the treasure was not for him. And yet, good heavens! a man like Ben Hall could never have invented a puzzle of the Captain Kidd order—as set down by Edgar Allan Poe in his story of the "Golden Beetle." That was a staggerer, and showed the gallant pirate to be a man of much ingenuity and no little erudition— which he may have been. But one thing was certain, Ben Hall was not, so that his puzzle must be simple by comparison. A bushranger's freak, that's what it was. No doubt Ben had, as a happy, guileless boy, read of pirates and buried treasures galore, so that when he came to man's estate, and had more gold than he knew exactly what to do with, he sought to emulate the doings of those worthy rovers. This cipher was the result, and it could not, it *could not* be anything but simple.

He knocked the ashes from his pipe and turned once more to the hut, but on the threshold stopped suddenly, a horrible doubt having crossed his mind. *Suppose the thing were a fraud!* For a moment he felt quite sick and giddy, and in that brief space entertained a series of truly harrowing thoughts. Yet only for a moment. There had been too many crimes committed for the possession of that paper to doubt its genuineness. No, it was true enough. It held a secret, a secret which must be his.

Once more he sat himself at his improvised table and began the dreary work, but he was not afraid of it this time, for he had convinced himself that it could not be such a terrible thing as he had previously been inclined to suppose. Now he despaired, now he hoped; yet when he seemed to have his hand on the thing, it slipped between his fingers. To make matters worse Phil here awoke, and, seeing his companion still poring over the papers, lit his pipe and began to smoke.

"Do you know what time it is, mate?" he asked.

"No—that is," said Vincent, looking at his watch, "it's half-past four."

"Ain't you going to turn in?"

"I don't know." And he set to work again, writing and muttering in an extraordinary manner.

Phil watched him in silence for a long time, a good-natured smile of pity on his rugged face.

"What is it, mate?" he asked at length.

"Confound you, dry up!" was the angry response, and the young fellow went on with his writings and his mutterings for a full minute longer, entirely oblivious of all around him. At last, looking up at the Reclaimed One, he said, "I beg your pardon, old man, but I had just caught an idea."

"You've had a mighty long chase, mate."

"Nothing like exercise, you know," laughed the young man.

"I get all I want during the daytime," said Mr. Phil. "But what's it all about, mate?"

"It's a sum, Phil, the answer of which I have been trying to work out."

"You don't mean to tell me that you're keeping out of your warm bed for the sake of doing a sum?"

"That's so."

The Brand opened wide his big brown eyes.

"Well, I'm blowed," he gasped, and sank back on his pillow with a sigh.

Vincent turned once more to the bewildering letters and worked on solidly for another half-hour. Then he began to wriggle nervously on his stool, his fingers trembled as the pencil flew over the paper, his breath came hard. Phil watched him curiously, eagerly. Certainly, by what that worthy remembered of arithmetic, he had never imagined there was anything in it half so entertaining. George, however, wholly unconscious of the interest he had awakened in his companion, sat staring fixedly at the paper. He had made a great discovery, or at least he thought he had. One thing was certain, he had formed all the letters into words, some of which were so familiar that he scarcely dared to credit his own eyes. Reading from left to right, beginning at the bottom and then continuing from the right-hand side of the fifth line, as though there were no break, and carrying out this plan with the lines above, he had, by taking every second letter, formed an incongruous series of words, which he at first thought was mere chance. But by the transposition of every second word also, and the insertion of a few marks of punctuation, the cipher became perfectly intelligible, and read as follows :

Step the letters. Morgan's last jaunt. Dead Man's Flat.

For a while he looked at these words in a thoroughly bewildered way, wondering, trembling lest they should not be the correct answer. But recollecting all that he had heard concerning the Mount Marong Escort, his doubts flew like dust before the wind.

"Eureka!" he cried, bounding to his feet. "I've got it."

"Got 'em you mean," cried the Reclaimed One, sitting up. "What's the matter now?"

George loooked round at his companion, feeling exceedingly embarrassed. So engrossed had he been with the study of this problem that he had entirely overlooked the fact that he was not alone. He wondered if he had betrayed his secret in any way, and turned a searching glance towards the worthy Brand, but the puzzled look in those big eyes showed clearly enough that his secret was safe in that direction.

"What is it, George?" repeated the man. "Anyone would think you had struck a big patch."

Vincent laughed, a little oddly, his companion thought.

"I've found the answer to my sum."

"Oh, lor, is that all! If I was you, mate, I'd take off my togs and tumble in for an hour or so. Sums are right enough in their way, I suppose, and good enough for schoolmasters, clerks and counter-jumpers, but I never see'd the sum yet that could keep me two minutes out of my bunk. Take my advice, George, and turn in. You look that scared that if I didn't know you I should think you had been on the drink for a week."

Vincent laughed again, but, instead of following Phil's parental advice, lit his pipe once more and stepped out into the cool night. Here he walked up and down till the grey light of the morning began to steal through the dark curtains of the east.

"Step the letters. Morgan's last jaunt. Dead Man's Flat." The words rang in his ears, burnt themselves upon his brain. One moment he was bursting with hope, the next plunged deep in despair. Suppose this should not be the right reading? This horrid thought gave birth to a dozen others, all equally terrifying. He paced the few yards before his tent with the impetuosity of a madman, now muttering and now again stopping to interrogate the morning star. And yet, in the midst of all this doubt and fear, he felt a certain sense of security in the knowledge that he had worked out his answer in a systematic manner. Had the letters been merely set down at random, or did they contain another systematically arranged cipher, it were ten thousand to one that he would not have succeeded as he had. Now, if this were the correct answer, and there was no reason why it should not be, the gold was as good as his, for the understanding of the words presented little difficulty. " Step the letters. Morgan's last jaunt "—undoubtedly meant that as there were forty-two letters in the cipher, you were to take that many steps, or paces, *from* Morgan's Last Jaunt (wherever, or whatever, that was), which would bring you in the neighbourhood of the treasure. It would indeed have been less difficult had the writer only mentioned in which direction you should step; but that was in itself a mere nothing. George felt equal to taking up the earth for a good hundred yards around that mystic spot. But first, what was Morgan's Last Jaunt? Was it the name of a place, or the name of a thing? This puzzled him not a little, for he never recollected hearing the expression. Yet, as the words plainly indicated, "Morgan's Last Jaunt" was at "Dead Man's Flat," and as the sticking-up of the Mount Marong Escort was a matter of history, he felt that a little judicious questioning of the "old identities" would quickly clear up this point.

Nor was that all. Six thousand ounces of gold was a large sum, and would require, should it ever be found, secret and expeditious handling. Now, could one man undertake such a task? True, Ben Hall had buried it, or was supposed to have buried it, alone, but there was no proof of this; besides, when he was at Dead Man's Flat it was a howling wilderness. Now thousands of men swarmed the Flat and its adjacent hills, and the police, mounted and on foot, patrolled the place day and night. Times were changed since Mr. Benjamin Hall paid his memorable visit to the then lonesome spot. One might have done anything with impunity in those days, for at that time there was no single habitation between Mount Marong and Gundalla, a distance of thirty-seven miles. Now there were numerous small townships along the route, for the fame of Dead Man's Flat had spread far and wide, and to the skirts of every famous thing you will find smaller things hanging.

Really, how to secure this treasure once it was found seemed, at the first glance, almost as great a problem as the cipher itself; but George, being somewhat practical in spite of his emotional nature, thought it would be just as well to find the gold first: and since it might come to pass that he would have to share his secret with another, why not forestall time's mandate by taking Phil into his confidence at once? That worthy one was on his best behaviour now; a Brand plucked from the Burning and quenched with tears of regret. Devoted heart and soul to Vincent, whom he looked upon as the saviour of his wife and child, the young fellow had experienced so many little tokens of his sincerity that he felt that he might trust him. Moreover, there was money to be gained (for he meant to reward him handsomely), money for his wife and child, and the young man knew that for their sakes alone Phil would keep his counsel and work like a slave.

He pushed back the flap of the tent and entered. Phil was sitting up in bed darning a sock.

"I'm afraid I have broken into your rest, Phil, old man."

"Not in the least," replied the Reclaimed One, pulling hard at his pipe. "Besides, it's nearly getting-up time; and I've had this blessed job on hand for over a week. Ah, mate, one misses the old woman when it comes to darnin', and sewin' and washin'. But ain't you goin' to turn in a bit? I think you ought 'er, you know. Sitting up all night over a bit of 'rithmetic is foolishness, George, downright foolishness."

"Suppose I could prove to you that it were not?"

"Then show me that it means L s. d."

"Suppose I can?"

"Going in for schoolmasterin'?"

"No."

"Nor clerkin', nor counter-jumperin'?"

"No, thank you. I've had enough of ledgers."

"Then I take it all back, mate, though I still argue that the night is the time for a man to sleep."

"Granted; but a man does not often get such a chance as this to keep him awake."

"You're mighty mysterious, mate. What is it?"

"Look here, Phil, can you keep a secret if I give you a thousand pounds for doing it?"

"I can keep a secret for nothing, if it's yours, mate."

"Thank you, Phil, but I have no intention of putting you to such a test. I think we understand each other, don't we?"

"That's so," said Phil. "Leastways, I know you to be the best mate I ever struck." And he returned to his darning, though it was evident by the way his needle wobbled that his hand had grown very shaky all of a sudden, or his eyes very dim.

"Then what I want, Phil, is a man who will help me, and keep my secret."

"That's me," said Phil, looking up from his darning. "I ain't forgot the missis, you know, nor the little 'un, and I'd like to show you that I mean what I say." There was a ring of pathos and sincerity in the man's rough voice which could not be mistaken. Vincent seized his hand and shook it warmly.

"I know I may trust you, Phil."

"To the last drop of my blood."

And Vincent knew he meant it.

"Then let me tell you," continued the young fellow, "that the sum I have been working at all night was no ordinary arithmetical problem."

"I thought you couldn't have been such a fool."

"Thanks for your good opinion. No:

I have got beyond working like that for the love of the thing. I have been trying to find out the answer to this puzzle."

Extracting the cipher from his pocket he handed it to his companion, who, after staring blankly at it for a few moments, returned it with a shake of his head.

"Well, what's it all about?"

"It's about a treasure which is secreted somewhere on Dead Man's Flat."

"What, that bit of letterin' is? Now how did you find that out?"

"It was a tough job as you saw, but I believe I've got hold of the right reading."

"And what is this treasure, mate?"

"Gold—heaps of it—thousands of pounds' worth."

"At Dead Man's Flat?" asked Phil incredulously, his big eyes opening till he seemed all eyes.

"Yes, at Dead Man's Flat."

"Oh, it's rot, you know," said the

Reclaimed One somewhat peevishly. "Look here, mate, you pull off your boots and tumble in for a couple of hours. You'll feel ever so much better presently."

George laughed loudly. "I'm all right, Phil. Haven't even lost a shingle," and he touched his forehead.

"Then who could have planted anything hereabouts?"

"Did you never hear of anyone making a big haul in these parts, many years ago?"

"Can't say that I have — except," he added, "Ben Hall."

"Exactly."

"Do you mean to say that you have found old Ben's Plant?"

"Not quite, but I shall—if you'll help me."

"Help you, of course. But, mate, it ain't a joke?"

"My share of it is not, and I think

you'll find a thousand yellow boys a joke of the right sort."

"That's so," said the man, "that's so. Polly shall have that new black silk, after all; and the little 'un, why I'll bring her up like a lady. Your hand, mate; it's a bargain."

"You swear that you won't betray me?"

"Before Gord!" exclaimed the man earnestly. "Trust me, that's all. I'm no great hand at speechifying, George, but I know what I mean. Put it there, mate. You can trust me as you would yourself."

Again the two men clasped hands, and with that silent oath their bond of comradeship was sealed. Then Vincent, sitting on Phil's bed, related to that worthy all that he knew concerning the cipher, beginning with the murder in Little Lonsdale Street, and ending with that night's mastery of the secret.

"Well," said Phil, "it's a mighty queer

story, old man, and you've come out of it pretty slick. But I can't understand how Logan should have tumbled to it."

"You will when I tell you that I believe Logan to be no other than Flash Jim."

"What! Jim Regan?"

"Precisely; and it was he, or his companion Smith, who broke into our place that night. They were in search of this little bit of paper."

"I believe you've struck it. But who is Smith?"

"I cannot say for certain, but I believe him to be Stephen Jones."

"Snaky Steve! — The cruellest of the gang."

"Such is my belief. Now you understand why I wanted a mate in this business. We have a couple of desperate scoundrels to deal with."

"That we have, and no mistake. But there's the police——"

"Not till *after* we have found the Plant."

"I understand. But we must keep our eyes skinned, matey. I'll go over to the town this afternoon and buy a new pistol. I can tell you what it is, George: If those two men are really Regan and Jones, the sooner we get hold of old Ben's Plant and clear, the better it will be for us."

"You may depend that we cannot find the gold too soon for me."

"No, I suppose not," said the Reclaimed One with a knowing smile.

"But there's something here I should like to speak to you about. Did you ever hear of 'Morgan's Last Jaunt'?"

"Morgan's Last Jaunt?" he repeated. "Morgan's la — Oh, you mean Morgan's Jaunt?"

"Yes, Morgan's Jaunt will do. What is it—where is it?"

"Morgan's Jaunt," said Mr. Phil, slowly, "is the big white gum tree down on the

Flat, where old Tommy and those bushmen he spoke of strung up Jack Morgan—one of Ben Hall's beauties. You can see a part of the rope round the big bough yet."

"Do you know this tree?"

"Lord bless you, yes. It was pointed out to me the first Sunday I came here. It's right alongside of the main road."

"Is it far from here?"

"Under a mile, I should say."

"Down the creek, of course?"

"Yes."

"Well, it's about there we must search for the treasure. Now, Phil, having told you all I know, I think I'll try and put in a couple of hours' sleep. No work to-day, old man. We'll go fossicking after breakfast.

Phil smiled pleasantly to himself as he contemplated the hole in his sock; then held it up to the light with a disdainful look, which said quite plainly, " I shall soon have done with the likes of you;" and then, having a present use for it, he set to with renewed assiduity. George, his face to the wall, or what should have been the wall, slept peacefully on, dreaming of the Mount Marong Escort and a pair of soft, grey eyes; while from the frowning crests of the far-eastern hills the heralds of the day-god sprang with feet of fire.

CHAPTER VIII.

MORGAN'S LAST JAUNT.

It was quite ten o'clock when George awoke. Surprised to see the sunshine streaming strongly through the door, he sprang hurriedly from his bed, calling to Phil to get some breakfast ready, and while that worthy busied himself preparing the meal, the young fellow made a rapid toilet.

After breakfast, which consisted principally of strong tea and bread and butter, the two men set off down the creek, one carrying a tin dish, the other a pick and shovel—the usual complement of the digger. They were going "fossicking" down the creek, they said, in answer to numerous enquiries; and so they were, but it was for a " patch " which would have set the whole camp in a ferment could it only have known.

To reach the Flat proper, however, it was first necessary to cross the creek, and this could only be done, especially at anything like high water, which it was now on account of the recent rains, by means of the bridge. But there was no sign to tell them of the dastardly crime the dark night had lately witnessed, and so they passed over the spot full of hope and pleasant dreams. Turning away to the left, they then followed the course of the creek for about half-a-mile, but from that point struck off across the Flat to the Mount Marong Road, and after pursuing that uninteresting highway for another half-mile, pulled up beneath the indifferent shade of a big white gum tree.

"This is what the old hands used to call Morgan's Jaunt," said Phil, nodding towards the tree, "though the name's gone out of date now, and you rarely hear it; but it was from that big bough, mate, that Jack Morgan took his Last Jaunt on earth. Look, there's a bit of the rope he dangled on."

He pointed to a great bough as he spoke, the lowest and largest of all, which shot out from the tree's trunk in the direction of the road. This huge limb could not have been less than twenty feet from the ground, and, near that portion of it where its first branch grew, might still be seen, encircling the prong, as it were, a piece of black, rotten rope. This had been a grim jaunt indeed, and as the young man stood picturing the scene he wondered what wag had perpetrated such a ghastly joke.

"Well," said he, turning to his companion, who with wide-open eyes was staring at the rope, and twisting his neck about in the most singular manner, "this is Morgan's

Jaunt right enough; but where is old Ben's Plant?"

"Ay, where?" answered the Reclaimed One, rubbing his neck with the back of his hand. "Besides, mate," he added, pointing in the direction of the camp, "we shall never be able to fossick round here without having the police down on us, not counting the prowlers, who are everywhere."

"It is a bit open, Phil; but once we know where to look for the gold, trust me to get it away."

Speaking thus, he fixed his back firmly against the tree, and then stepped forty-two paces in a northerly direction; but this brought him to a little rocky hill, or elevation, a few minutes' examination of which proving conclusively that Ben had not hidden his treasure there. This was not an encouraging start, for if Vincent had been going to do as Ben did, this little elevation, back from the road as it was, and beyond the ken of the passer-by, would have been the place of places he would have chosen. Then he stepped forty-two paces eastward, but this landed him in a little gully along which countless diggers had passed with pick and shovel. Still he was not to be denied, and for quite an hour he and Phil swung pick and shovel in vain.

"No go," said George, with a nervous little laugh. "Let us try to westward."

Shouldering their implements they turned about, but on looking up the gully beheld the well-known and equally well-detested form of Mr. Samuel Smith.

"Hallo," cried Phil, "there's Snaky Steve watching us. What's he up to?"

"No good, you may depend."

"Let us watch him."

With that the two men began to mount the gully, at which Mr. Smith, seeing he was observed, at once proceeded to make himself scarce. When George and his companion reached the level ground, that amiable gentleman was nowhere to be seen.

"Gone like a spirit," said Phil; "disappeared into the bosom of his father the devil."

"Let us hope so. But come, we have yet two sides to try."

They then retraced their steps to the big tree, and George again stepped the forty-two paces, this time to the westward; but here the opposition he had met in the north again encountered him, for the patch of rock extended in this direction to within a lew yards of the roadway.

"Well," said he, stopping a moment to wipe the perspiration from his forehead, "we have only one more main point, Phil. I'm afraid we shall have to trench round this old tree at a distance of from forty to fifty yards."

"I wouldn't mind that," said Phil boldly,

"if we were only sure of our ground. Though I'd like to know how you expect to be allowed to do the job?"

"Buy the land, of course."

"Of course; but if I'm not mightily mistaken, mate, that road there ain't fifty yards from this old gum, and I'd like to know," he added somewhat severely, "how you're going to buy the main road?"

"Well, let us measure it first and discuss our plans afterwards." So saying, he once more planted his back against the tree, and again stepped the required number of paces, drawing up within a few yards of the road. The two men looked at each other blankly; Phil smiled in a silly sort of way, while George grew very nervous.

"I suppose this road was here when Hall stuck-up the Mount Marong Escort?" he asked.

"And long before then," was the reply.

"It was along this very road the Escort came, and it was from behind those very bushes," he pointed to some trees and shrubs about half-a-mile away, " that Hall's men fired on the troopers."

"Then this is a most unlikely spot in which to bury a treasure. Let us try the different points of the compass."

"Well," said the Brand, as they walked despondently back to the tree, " it don't seem to me the sort of place a cute 'un like Ben would bury anything in—unless it was a trooper," he added jocularly. There was a grim humour about Mr. Phil which was vastly entertaining.

So they walked slowly back, Mr. Phil full of the 'cuteness of Ben, and Mr. George just a little distressed and anxious. But all of a sudden Mr. Phil grew nervous too, and began to tremble strangely. He uttered no exclamation, but his breath came in quick gasps. And the reason? A brilliant idea had struck him; but as it was the first time on record such a misfortune had befallen him, he was afraid to speak of it. Yet when they regained the shade of the tree, he stood with his mouth wide open, staring up at the great bough and the bit of black rope.

"What are you looking at?" asked Vincent. "One would think you could see Morgan's ghost."

"I ain't so sure that I can't, mate," was the reply, "for I can see an idea."

"An idea," laughed George.

"Ay. If you was to stand *under* this bit of rope and measure forty-two paces, where would it lead you?"

"It all depends on the direction."

"There's only one direction, mate," and he pointed to the road.

"That's it," said Vincent, "it would lead me on the road."

"Try, mate."

George stood under the spot where the bushranger had dangled, which was some five or six yards from the trunk of the tree, and then deliberately stepped the required number of paces, which carried him fair into the middle of the road.

"Well," he laughed, "I'm afraid this won't do. It's not likely to be beneath the public highway, is it?"

"Why not?"

George looked round quickly, surprised at the words and the serious tone; but he was even more surprised at the serious look in his companion's face. The meaning of that look struck him in a moment, and with force too. Like an inspiration it came; strong as a blow. His breath came with a sudden leap to his throat.

"Why not," he repeated, "yes, why not?"

"I'm glad you see it in that way, mate. If all I've heard of Ben Hall was true, it is the very place of places he would have chosen. What safer spot could be found than this? Of all the thousands who ever tramped this road, do you suppose one of them ever thought of a treasure beneath his feet?"

"I suppose not."

"Why," continued Phil, waxing warm, "the more I think of it the more cunning it strikes me, and, mind you, old Ben was a mighty cute 'un. It's simple enough, to be sure, but it's these simple things that upset a man's calculations. He knew a thing or two, did Ben. You see, George, this is the main road between Mount Marong and Gundalla, and as such will always be kept in repair and safe from the picks and shovels of the builder and the fossicker."

"It's a capital idea," said George.

"It's just what Ben would have done, and you take my word for it, if this treasure is to be found anywhere, its here under our feet." And as he spoke Mr. Phil stamped loudly on the dusty road.

"I have no wish to believe other than that, and can see no reason why I should. All that remains now is for us to prove the truth, or otherwise, of the idea. In the meantime, we must think out how best we may set to work. Have you any suggestion to make?"

"We might try and get a job road-making," suggested Phil.

"Or pipe-laying, eh?" laughed his companion.

"I don't see anything to laugh at, mate. If you can think of something better I shall be quite willing to see it out. One thing is certain; we can't pull up the road, can we?"

"I suppose not. We should have the patrol down on us."

"Patrol!" exclaimed Mr. Phil, "I should think so, and swag-men and mail-coaches, and the Lord knows what not. No, mate, we shall have to peg out a claim as near to the road as they'll allow us, and then drive under till we reach the plant."

" Not a bad idea, Phil, but just a little too open—and laborious."

" Then what do you suggest ? "

" I suggest that we think the matter over till to-night. By that time we may have gathered a few ideas."

" It strikes me we are sadly in need of them. But are you going into the town ? "

" Yes."

" Would you mind getting me that pistol ? "

" Ha, ha ! You mean business, Phil ? "

" You bet I do," said Mr. Phil, grimly. " That thousand pounds is going into the bank in the missis's name, and I'm going to bring up my little 'un like a lady."

" That thousand shall be doubled, old

fellow, and there's my hand to the bargain."

Phil looked at the young man in a glad, wondering sort of way. Then seizing his hand pressed it in a vice-like grip. " I wouldn't take it, mate," he said in a quivering voice, " if it wasn't for them. But they'll be happy, won't they, and never fear the landlord any more, and the little 'un won't go to bed cryin' of hunger? If my life's blood can pay you back, mate, it's yours whenever you want it."

" Let us be friends, Phil, that's all."

So they took up their prospecting implements and retraced their steps towards the camp, parting at the bridge, Phil to go back to his dreams and his darning, George to make his way to the " Emu's Head."

With a strange quiver at his heart, for which he could not account — having determined to meet Logan on the same familiar footing—the young fellow entered the well-known door, and from thence passed on to the little private parlour at the back of the bar. To him the house seemed strangely, almost oppressively, still, though, as it was then the quietest part of the day, the stillness might be somewhat accounted for. It surprised him, however, to hear no sound of voice nor tramp of foot. It was not a bit like the " Emu's Head."

He peeped through the partly-opened door into the bar, in the far corner of which he saw Edith sitting, her head thrown wearily back against the counter, her eyes half-closed, a strange, tired look upon her face. Whether she was asleep, or fainting, or dreaming, he could not say; but he was so startled at the sight of her white, sad face, that he could not suppress the cry which rose to his lips. Hearing him, she bounded to her feet.

"Ah, you have come, you have come!"

"Yes, darling," he answered, drawing her into the little room as he spoke. "But you, you look ill?"

"I am not ill," she said, "only tired, fatigued — and perhaps a little bit frightened."

"Frightened?"

"Of nothing," she said with a nervous laugh, nestling closer to him.

"What is the matter, dear? Is there anything I can do for you?"

"Be as you are," she replied. "That is all I want."

"I shall be always that, darling, never fear. But it is this house that affects you, is it not? You will never be happy here, Edith?"

"No," she said, "I do not think I shall."

"Courage," he whispered fondly, "your release may now be counted by hours."

And then he told her how he had read the puzzle, and how he hoped soon to lay his hands on the gold.

"But why do I find you here again?" he asked. "This is entirely against my agreement with your cousin."

"Poor Kitty is not well to-day."

"Have you seen her?"

"No; but I heard through Bridget."

"And Logan?"

"He, too, is unwell. He sent to ask if I would mind looking after the place till he came down. Of course, I couldn't refuse."

"I suppose not, but I don't like it, all the same. Never mind, darling. Keep up your courage for a little while longer. If all goes as I fondly hope, and, really, I do not see why it should not, the hour of your emancipation is very, very near."

At that moment steps were heard outside in the passage, and George had only time to withdraw his hands from her shoulders when the burly Logan entered. Upon seeing Vincent he looked, for the moment, both surprised and nervous, but being a man of varied experience, he knew how to hide both, which he did, on this occasion, beneath a familiar grin.

"Ha, ha! At it again!" he cried in his pleasantest manner. "Well, as I said before, you must go it while you're young, you know," and he laughed again in his own familiar way. "Thank you, Edith," he said, as he waddled into the bar, "I have come to relieve you."

George led the girl out into the passage.

"You look faint," he said. "Go and have some tea, and then lie down for a couple of hours."

"Yes, I will. But did you notice how ghastly *he* looked?"

"Yes. I suppose he has been on the drink again, the scoundrel."

"Heaven only knows. But I cannot, I cannot bear the sight of him."

"No wonder. But courage, darling. It is only for a little while longer; and Kitty has promised to guard you with her life."

What passed between them then, we need not be too curious to know; hut it is certain that the colour came back to her cheeks in a wonderful manner, and that when he stepped forth from the "Emu's Head" he felt like a hero of fairy lore — capable of mighty deeds.

CHAPTER IX.

HALL'S PLANT.

He, however, had no sooner cleared the town than he observed a series of great black clouds come rolling up sullenly from the west, sending the angry sun down in a chaos of whirling mist. That a storm was brewing was most apparent, for there was a low, monotonous hum in the rapidly darkening air which could only have been caused by some far-off elemental warfare. Knowing the extreme suddenness with which such storms descend, Vincent put his right foot foremost and sped rapidly onward. Yet, when he reached the bridge which spanned the creek, he stood for a moment to watch the setting of the sun.

And a strange going down it was. Like some great, yet furious, spirit, the vast globe of fire sullenly withdrew behind its black-green curtains, through which it lowered lurid and awful. Yet down, down it went, its defiant beams darting forth and piercing those sombre forms with a momentary radiance, then instantly fading into nothingness. And still the clouds grew more intense, more black, pressing down, as it were, the sullen globe, which one moment asserted itself in a blaze of glory, then disappeared behind the earth. At the same moment a great streak of lightning darted across the world, and from out the bosom of the chaotic mass of could a groan went forth—a mighty peal of thunder. Vincent clung fast to the bridge, for the whole world seemed to be shaken by that angry roar. Then flash succeeded flash, the lightning treading a mazy whirl on its soft black carpet of cloud.

So vivid was it that he stood bewildered, shading his eyes with his hand, his brain ringing with the noise of the thunder. Then a dozen great drops of rain fell pat-pat upon him, and not wishing to be washed away by the deluge which was sure to follow, he took to his heels, nor stopped till he reached the equivocal shelter of his tent.

And yet he need not have hurried himself, unless it were to escape the lightning. For two full hours the dangerous sparks flew hither and thither, lighting the premature darkness with a weird glory. And all this time the rain held off, or only fell in big solitary drops at odd intervals. It seemed as though the sheet of fire which hung continually in the heavens had sucked up all the moisture. But, as the lightning diminished, the darkness began to groan again, and the reverberations shook the world. Crash!—and then with a long-drawn roar, which seemed to gain strength and volume as on it sped, the peal ran shrieking across the globe. Such a blast shall the Archangel blow when he wakes the dead from their long sleep.

With the thunder came the rain, so vehemently, that it seemed as though God had repented of his promise. In sheets it fell—hissing, roaring, drenching sheets. Time after time Vincent and his companion turned with anxious looks to the delicate roof above them, which, so far, had held nobly, though at what moment the wild water would burst through, no man might say.

"A bad night," exclaimed Phil for the hundredth time, as though he had just been struck with a brilliant idea, "a devil of a night. Do you think she'll hold?" This of the roof, to which he pointed with the candle in the intervals of lighting his pipe.

"I shouldn't like to swear by her," was the moody reply.

"No, nor me."

Then there was silence between the two for several moments, both pulling steadily at their pipes and watching the roof with anxious faces.

"Good lord!" exclaimed Phil as a sudden gust of wind brought on a vicious downpour which almost burst in the canvas, "that was a beauty, wasn't it?"

"Another like that and away she'll go," said Vincent consolingly, referring to the drenched canvas. "We might turn in if it wasn't for that most probable contingency."

"Um!" grunted the Reclaimed One, "it's a devil of a night and no mistake."

Then silence fell upon them once more, and they sat in their bunks smoking as though their lives depended upon their consuming a certain quantity of the fragrant weed. Outside the wind howled like a legion of demons, and the rain came swish, swish against their frail canvas, making it quiver and creak ominously.

At last Phil broke the silence. He had evidently been thinking of his wife and child, for he said with a sigh, " Gord help the poor."

" Amen."

" They need it mate, eh, when the landlord's down on 'em, and the nights is like this ? "

" Yes. But it's strange how even the poorest can find a shelter."

" That's true. I daresay if you went through the camp now you wouldn't find a soul stirring. Even the police'll be under cover weather like this. You know," added Mr. Phil knowingly, " a drop of toddy and a quiet game of cards."

" The very thing," cried Vincent bounding to his feet.

"No, not for me," exclaimed the Reclaimed One hastily. "I've sworn off."

George laughed. "I didn't mean that, you old duffer. I mean that it's the very night for us to take up the road."

Phil leapt from his bunk with a mighty oath.

"So it is. By the Lord, a grand idea! There won't be a soul abroad. The mail was due two hours ago; and as for the patrol—it'll know better than come that far on such a night."

"But suppose some new arrivals come along?"

"No fear—not this sort of weather."

"But a vehicle—a waggon?"

"Waggons are driven by human beings, and human beings ain't ducks," said Mr. Phil facetiously. "Besides, if one does come along I'll manage that business quick enough. Road's dangerous — you understand?" · This with a comprehensive wink. "I'm there to show them the way."

"My dear Phil, you are a man of infinite resource."

"Then don't let us waste another moment."

With that they proceeded to put on their big high boots and greatcoats, George slipping a flask of whisky and water in his pocket. Phil seized the pick and shovel, his companion the lantern and three extra candles, also two stout sacks, which they hoped would prove invaluable. Thus equipped the pair stepped out into the storm.

At first the wind howled so dreadfully and the rain descended in such torrents that they stood irresolute; but quickly picking up their bearings, in spite of the intense blackness of the night, they started forth, cautiously feeling their way; and through the dark, rain-drenched camp they went, now slipping, sprawling, and, I am ashamed to say, occasionally swearing like the proverbial trooper.

At last they reached the road which led to the bridge (for by a circuitous route had they advanced lest some too officious trooper should be doing his duty), and a few minutes after they trod that shaky structure. For a moment George stood to gaze down upon the roaring water, which foamed so that it looked grey in the darkness; but the restless Phil was immediately at his elbow and away they went once more. And all this time the rain came down as though it would never cease, blinding them with its fury, drenching them to the skin. Yet, in spite of the strenuous opposition of the elements, they plodded sturdily on, for when a strong man determines it shall go hard with him before he cries enough!

At last they reached the tree with the

grimly humorous name, and once more stepping the forty-two paces, found themselves in the middle of the muddy road. Then George, to make quite certain of his bee line, stood Phil on the road while he once more retraced his steps to the tree. Here he again took up his position beneath the piece of rope, and from where he stood he could see the lantern dead before him, so, feeling certain that the direction was the true one, he hurriedly rejoined his mate.

"Out with the light, Phil, we don't want the police down on us." In a moment the lantern was extinguished, and George, seizing the shovel, began to clear away the mud.

"You stand back a bit, Phil," he continued, " and keep your eyes and ears open. When I want a spell I'll call you." And Phil did as he was told, while Vincent worked on, oblivious of the pelting rain.

It was a task undertaken with every disadvantage, but, notwithstanding the storm and the darkness, George worked on like a veritable Trojan, and soon had the satisfaction of opening a trench quite two feet deep, some five feet wide, and between six and eight in length. Then he called Phil to his side, and that worthy, throwing off his sodden great-coat, jumped into the hole, and began to work away with superhuman energy.

Calling Vincent to him after a quarter of an hour's hard work, he said, "I think we might try the light now."

George bore the lantern up to the big tree for shelter, lit it and brought it back.

"Well," said he in a nervous voice, as he handed his mate the light, "how does the ground feel?"

"We're on it, mate, that's how it feels," cried Phil excitedly.

"You are sure?"

"As sure as a man can be. I've sunk too many holes in my day not to know what I'm talking about." And with a grunt he dug the pick into the yielding earth.

George went back to his beat—which consisted of a promenade of about fifty yards on either side of his companion—in a perfect whirl of excitement. Every pulse within him seemed to beat in unison with the wild night, beat, beat, till at times he trembled on the verge of a delirium. What would be the result of this undertaking? A thousand times he asked himself this question, and a thousand times trembled to reply. And all the while the rain descended as though the flood gates of heaven had been thrown open; the wind howled dismally as it tore through the black night; he was drenched to the skin, and the mud clung to his big boots, turning them into huge mounds of earth. Yet he seemed to feel none of these inconveniences, for in the darkness there was light, and in the light a pair of soft grey eyes. He seemed to think only of her, and prized the treasure only because it would bring her to him. That sad, pale face of hers had haunted him of late; those wistful eyes with their appealing glances seemed to reproach him with a thousand mute utterances.

Presently he was recalled to the things of earth by hearing Phil hail him; but rushing over suddenly he discovered that that worthy merely wished to be relieved. Into the hole the young fellow immediately sprang and was both surprised and delighted to find that his companion had deepened the excavation by nearly three feet. With almost superhuman vigour Vincent again set to, and after descending another foot he began to work excitedly, for he had come across a piece of thick bark—a thing which could not have been found there if this part of the road had never been touched! But this surprise was almost immediately followed by a still greater one. Suddenly his pick struck against another object, sending the strangest sensation through every limb. It seemed as though the instrument had entered wood! For a moment he stood quite still, his heart thumping so that his sides could scarce contain it. Then of a sudden he fell down on his knees and began to scoop out the soil with his hands, and presently he laid bare a piece of partly-decayed wood. He could scarcely believe his eyes, credit his senses. He held the lantern close to the object he had unearthed. and there, sure enough, was a piece of wood bound with an iron band!

"It's the gold boxes," he cried aloud in his great joy, "hurrah!"

Phil, hearing the shout, ran up.

"What is it, mate?"

"The Plant!"

"No!"

"Look, then!"

In a moment Phil was in the hole beside him. "So it is," he said in an awed whisper, "it is, by the Lord!"

George, in the meantime, much too excited to speak, continued to shovel out the earth which surrounded the box, an undertaking requiring no little pains, as the light was an indifferent one, and he did not wish to destroy the boxes, which he guessed would be half rotten by this time. So, proceeding with the utmost caution, he at length removed a sufficient quantity of the earth to allow him to use his pick as a lever, which doing, he soon had the satisfaction of seeing a small square box arise. Stooping down he seized it with both hands, and though it was only some eighteen inches long by nine broad, it was so heavy that he had to exert himself to draw it out from its earthy bed. But drawn out it was and handed to Phil, who made some jocular allusion to its weight and then, like Oliver Twist, asked for more. And more was duly forthcoming, for the withdrawal of the first box had laid bare more of a similar size, all iron-bound and of the same weight. There were ten of them altogether, and their weight could not have been less than fifty pounds each; so that, reckoning each box to contain fifty pounds' weight of gold, there could not have been less than five hundred pounds of that precious metal, the value of which would be, roughly speaking, between twenty and twenty-five thousand pounds sterling—a haul for the gods.

After digging about for some minutes in the vain hope of finding more, Vincent was constrained to confess that they had unearthed the whole of old Ben's treasure; so leaping from the pit he hurriedly began to fill it in, while Mr. Phil busied himself removing the boxes to the foot of Morgan's Jaunt. Here he mounted guard over the precious, if somewhat musty, collection, till his companion rejoined him.

"There," exclaimed that young gentleman, as he loomed up out of the darkness, the pick and shovel on his shoulder, "the job's done, and by the time the morning comes the rain will have washed away every trace of our undertaking. Now Phil, old man, what do you say to Ben Hall's Plant?"

"It seems almost too good to be true," was the reply of the Reclaimed One. "I can hardly believe yet that it's gold in all these boxes."

"Well," said Vincent a little startled, for the thought came home to him with a suddenness he did not appreciate, "I can't say myself that it's gold, old man, but we'll soon see." So taking up the pick he quickly prized one of the boxes open, discovering a stout canvas bag sealed with red wax. To break this seal and cut the binding was the work of a moment, and, by the flickering light of the lantern, they both saw that the bag was full of little nuggets of gold.

"That looks like the real thing," said Vincent triumphantly.

"Ay," was the awed response. "It's a great fortune, mate."

"It is, Phil; and a great weight too," laughed the young fellow.

"I think we could put up with a weightier inconvenience," suggested the Reclaimed One.

"I think so. But the next question is, how are we going to move it?"

Phil, ever imaginative, suggested a wheelbarrow; but George thought that that extremely useful, though perhaps undignified, vehicle, would scarcely be secret enough, and in turn suggested that they should make alternate journeys, a suggestion to which Mr. Phil immediately acquiesced. Luckily, by this time the rain was falling less heavily, and through a rift in the clouds could be seen the faint glimmer of a star.

Phil undertook the first journey, carrying, in one of the sacks George had brought, two of the boxes. He first of all tried three, but quickly coming to the conclusion that such a weight would only hinder him in the long run, he decided on the even number. He was quite half an hour on this journey, and during the whole of that time Vincent walked rapidly up and down beneath the gallows bough to keep up his circulation. That half-hour seemed to him the longest he had ever known, and he began to entertain doubts of Phil ever returning, but at the due expiration of that period the Reclaimed One stumbled back through the darkness reporting that all was well. Then he in turn loaded George in a similar manner, and away that worthy trudged, while the Brand, pulling vigorously at his pipe, began his sentry duty. Yet the half-hour that Vincent was away seemed to him an eternity, while to make matters worse he began to tremble and shiver so violently that he feared he had contracted some serious illness; indeed, when George returned he found the poor fellow in a most alarming state. A good pull at the whisky flask, however, produced a most surprising effect, and with a rather shaky laugh the redoubtable Phil declared he felt as well as ever. To this rash statement George paid little heed, and when poor Phil expressed a wish to go forth with another load, his companion made it known that they would journey together.

"But there will be two boxes left," said Phil.

"We'll put them in the bushes yonder, and I can come back for them after."

"As you will," was the reply. "To tell you the truth, mate, I feel a bit knocked up."

They then seized the boxes and carried them into the bit of scrub, some fifty yards away, and returning to the big tree took up the four that remained and set out on their journey.

To Vincent it seemed that those two boxes were laden with twice their imagined weight, while to poor Phil they seemed to outweigh a ton. Yet on he struggled gallantly, and though he fell twice, and had to rest several times, he persevered doggedly till the tent was reached. Then his strength gave way completely, and with a groan he fell to the floor. George, lighting a candle, was quickly by his side, and the whisky flask was again called into requisition. In a few moments Phil opened his big eyes in a wondering sort of way.

"Well," he exclaimed, with a pathetic little laugh, "I'm as weak as a blessed kid."

"The drenching has given you a severe cold. You must turn in now, old man, and try and get up a little warmth. You'll be all right again in the morning."

"I don't believe," chattered the poor fellow, " that I shall ever get warm again."

"Trust me," said the young man cheerfully, "I'll see to that." And he immediately proceeded to pull off his companion's wet clothes, a proceeding which caused poor Phil no little amusement, though there was something very pathetic in his repetition of the phrase, "blessed kid." George next rubbed him well with a coarse towel, and tucked him away in bed, telling him he would be as right as rain in the morning, though the poor fellow's teeth continued to chatter horribly, and the great shivers which swept from his head to his feet fairly shook the bunk.

"Are you going back for the other boxes?" he asked.

"Yes; unless you would rather I remained with you."

"No, no," he chattered, "only I'm afraid you might get this d——d shivering on you. Give me my pistol there. Put it under my pillow. Leave the candle alight, like a good chap. I'll watch till you come back."

"You are sure you don't mind me going?"

"Lord, no!" chattered the poor fellow. "What do you take me for?"

George then did as he was bidden; told the invalid to keep well covered up; gave him a final tuck-in, and then passed out into the night.

CHAPTER X.

INTO THE GREAT BEYOND.

It was with a feeling of extreme nervousness that George turned his back upon the hut, nor was that feeling allayed when he beheld a figure slink from before him and disappear behind one of the tents hard by; but, laughing the foolish superstition down, he strode rapidly onward. Again he crossed the ricketty bridge, beneath which the floodwater roared and hissed like a thousand demons; then passed spectre-like across the Flat to Morgan's Jaunt, and singularly lonely that gruesome spot seemed to him as he approached it, and he was not sure that he could not see the ghost of the departed bushranger dangling from the rotten rope. This pleased him not. He feared that he too might, in some inexplicable way, be suffering from excitement and the drenching he had received; and so, averting his face from the fatal bough, he made for the bushes where he had secreted the gold, discovered it, slung it upon his back, and immediately began his homeward journey.

Fortunately the rain had now ceased entirely, but the night was still very dark and the road over which he plodded was nothing better than a quagmire. Yet on he pushed with much determination, though he felt ill and weak, and seemed to bear the weight of the world upon his back. Now he slipped and staggered from side to side, and now he stumbled, as though intent upon measuring his length in the mud; yet on he pushed, resting at intervals, till the haven loomed in view. He was much surprised to see no gleam of light issue through the cracks of the flap, but supposed Phil had wished to go to sleep and so had blown out the candle. His surprise, however, gave way to an entirely different feeling when he discovered that the flap itself, which he had so carefully buckled, was undone.

With a heart that beat painfully, for terrifying were the suspicions which rushed in upon him, he hastily entered the tent. All there was dark and still. He stood listening for a moment—five—ten—but no sound reached his ears—only the low wailing of the wind as it swept through the air above. With a trembling hand he lit a match, and by its indistinct glare saw Phil lying, apparently asleep, and the figure of a man stretched out, face downwards, on the floor.

"Phil! Phil!" he cried hoarsely, "what's this?"

A low groan from the bunk was the only reply: at the same moment the match went out. With fingers that trembled even more, he instantly struck another, and perceiving the candle on the floor, by the foot of the man, whom he immediately recognised, he seized and lit it. Holding this close to his mate's face, he was horrified at its unearthly pallor.

"Phil! Phil!" he cried passionately, "speak, man, for God's sake, speak!" And as he spoke he lifted the dying man's head and poured a little stimulant down his throat. This had an almost instantaneous effect. The man's pallid eyelids quivered convulsively, then presently opened wide. A ghastly smile flickered across his wan face, but he uttered no word.

"Can you speak to me, Phil? What does it mean? How did it come about?"

The pale lips moved as though they would answer, but only a low, sibillant sound escaped them. A flash of anger shot from those big, dull eyes: the poor fellow evidently wished to speak. George had recourse once more to the whisky, and after forcing a strong dose through those pale lips, the glazed eyes brightened with something like the old fire.

"I was half dozing when he entered," the words came slowly and brokenly, as though each syllable cost a painful effort, "but I saw him and let him have it, though I wasn't strong enough to keep him off. You see, that d——d shivering had made me as weak as a kitten."

"Poor old Phil. Are you much hurt?"

"No, mate, not much—I'm only dying. You see, he knifed me here in the breast."

George turned back the man's shirt, which already bore a great crimson patch, and saw that the murderer's knife had made a ragged wound in the poor fellow's side. Phil saw the look of despair that mantled the young man's face.

"It's a bad one, ain't it?" he said, with a sad smile. "But it don't pain, mate; it's quite dead."

"Dead!"

"Ay, as a door-nail. And I'm about cooked too, I guess, for I feel the same sort o' coldness creepin' up over my body. It will touch me sharp in a minute, and then it'll be all over. But tell me, mate, what'll become of the missis and the little 'un when the old man's gone?"

Vincent took his cold hand and pressed it gently.

"They shall be my care," he said, his voice and eyes full of tears. "They shall never want while I have bread."

The dying man pressed his companion's hand endearingly. The tears rushed in a torrent to his eyes, blurring the little light that was left them.

"Gord bless you, mate, for those good words. I ain't afraid to go now, I ain't afraid to go. I know I was always a fool, but I was never a downright bad 'un, was I? And I was true to you, wasn't I? And I did keep my word, mate, didn't I? And though they jeered at me and called me the Reclaimed One, I stuck to it like a man, didn't I? You must tell the missis that— Poor, poor Polly! Tell her also that I wouldn't have given her little finger for the best of 'em, and that I was going to be a new man if Gord had only given me another chance. And don't forget to say she must have that black silk dress I promised to buy her when I came back from the diggings. I shan't come back, mate, but tell her I thought of her, won't you?"

Vincent pressed the cold hand in affirmation. He could not speak. The words would have choked him.

"And there's the little 'un, too," went on the poor fellow, in a low, fast-sinking voice; "tell her I meant to buy her that big doll we saw one day in George Street—and the silk dress—and the nice big pearl necklace with the gold clasps. Tell her—that—I——" The rest was lost in his throat. George felt the head grow suddenly heavy, the body stiffen. Phil was dead.

Vincent could have cried aloud, so great was his anguish—had it not been for that other presence. In losing Phil he had lost his only friend. For three long months they had lived and worked together, and he had learned to admire his mate's good qualities as well as condemn his bad ones. So it had all ended thus. A few hours ago he was a strong, hopeful man, full of good resolutions and thoughts as high as his quality of mind could soar. Now there could be nothing more on earth for him, except the narrow six feet which most of us may get. With the tears blurring his vision, the young man took a long, long look at those pale, calm features; then gently drew the blanket across the dead man's face.

He now turned his attention to the individual on the floor, whom he had already recognised as the man Smith, and whom he thought quite dead; but turning him on his back, and discovering there was yet a little life left in the fellow, his charity forbade him to let it run out without an effort at preservation. He therefore treated him to a stiff dose of whisky and water, which, though it eventually brought the life back, very nearly extinguished it at the time. The man's breath came in little hard gasps at first, then into a steady and more regular breathing. Presently he opened wide his eyes in a dazed manner, but the sight of the face above him quickly brought the light of consciousness into them.

"You?" he muttered, the word coming

big doll we saw one day in George Street—
and the silk dress—and the nice big pearl
necklace with the gold clasps. Tell her—
that—I——" The rest was lost in his
throat. George felt the head grow suddenly heavy, the body stiffen. Phil was
dead.

Vincent could have cried aloud, so great
was his anguish—had it not been for that
other presence. In losing Phil he had lost his
only friend. For three long months they
had lived and worked together, and he had
learned to admire his mate's good qualities
as well as condemn his bad ones. So it
had all ended thus. A few hours ago he
was a strong, hopeful man, full of good
resolutions and thoughts as high as his
quality of mind could soar. Now there
could be nothing more on earth for him,
except the narrow six feet which most of
us may get. With the tears blurring his
vision, the young man took a long, long

look at those pale, calm features; then gently drew the blanket across the dead man's face.

He now turned his attention to the individual on the floor, whom he had already recognised as the man Smith, and whom he thought quite dead; but turning him on his back, and discovering there was yet a little life left in the fellow, his charity forbade him to let it run out without an effort at preservation. He therefore treated him to a stiff dose of whisky and water, which, though it eventually brought the life back, very nearly extinguished it at the time. The man's breath came in little hard gasps at first, then into a steady and more regular breathing. Presently he opened wide his eyes in a dazed manner, but the sight of the face above him quickly brought the light of consciousness into them.

"You?" he muttered, the word coming

from his livid lips with a gasping effort. Vincent nodded affirmatively.

"You've got it, eh?"

"You mean Hall's Plant?"

"Yes." Again George nodded.

"Was the puzzle a hard one?" asked the man eagerly. Though evidently on the brink of the other world, with speech given to him for a moment or two before he was launched on the great journey, he seemed only to think of the treasure he had lost.

"I thought so at first," was Vincent's reply to his query, "but it seems to me now the simplest of things. You, however, should be thinking of something else. Have you anything to say? Can I do anything for you?"

"Yes, mate. Just sit there and tell me all about the Plant. There's nothing else you can do for me. I'm as good as gone. Your mate got the pull on me a bit too quick. If that fat cur had only stood by we'd have done it like clockwork."

"You mean Logan—as he calls himself?"

The man smiled in a ghastly way about the corners of his pale lips. "Yes, Flash Jim. He always was a cur, curse him. It was only because he was a gentleman, and useful as a spy, that old Ben had any truck with him. When we were about to stick-up the Mount Marong Escort he got so nervous that Ben wouldn't trust him with a gun, the cur. Ah, how we chaffed him. 'Jim Regan,' says Ben, 'you're a disgrace to this noble brotherhood. You haven't the heart of a jelly-fish, and if you wasn't such a dashed gentlemen, and such a favourite with the ladies—whom I wouldn't offend for the world, God bless 'em—I'd string you up alongside of old Jack Morgan.' Ah," sighed the man plaintively, "he was a rum dog was old Ben." His eyes remained closed during the recital of this incident put eliciting the fact that the aggressor was no other than Stephen Jones, otherwise known to fame as Snaky Steve, the wonder at the tragedy grew less. They had a business-like way of conducting affairs at Dead Man's Flat.

CHAPTER XI.

WHICH CONCLUDES THE CHRONICLE.

THAT George should sleep well through the remainder of that night was scarcely to be expected, but he nevertheless succeeded in snatching a few minutes here and there from the long hours. He was not afraid of ghosts, never having seen the like, but he often thought he could see his mate Phil lying over over there in the empty berth, and he could have sworn that he heard him sigh at least a dozen times. Then the guardianship of the vast treasure plagued him sorely. If by any chance it should be known that he had so great a sum in his keeping, he doubted if his life would be worth an hour's purchase; while last, though by no means least, there was Edith to fill his brain with further anxious thoughts. Smith's words about the woman, for whom he expressed sorrow, perplexed him greatly, and had his business with the police not lasted so long he would there and then have betaken himself off to the " Emu's Head "; but fearing to alarm her, he decided to await the morning.

Never were the first grey shades of day welcomed more by invalid than they were by him that morning, and as soon as there was light enough for him to dress by, he sprang from his bunk and hastily donned his clothes.

It was something to feel that the long, dangerous night was passed and that day was come once more; and it was with a feeling of inexpressible relief that he stepped outside into the early light. But this feeling of gladness was of short duration. He had not been many minutes contemplating the early sunrise before his attention was drawn to a little processsion which slowly approached him. It consisted of a horse and cart—upon the frontboard of which was perched a young gentleman smoking a short clay pipe—and two mounted troopers. The police rode close together, and seemed just a little more serious than is the wont of that callous brood, which made George imagine that there was something exceptional in or about that cart, in spite of the seeming nonchalance of its driver.

"Well, Jack," he shouted to the nearest trooper, as the cavalcade came abreast of him, "what's the matter now?"

The procession halted and George advanced.

"It's murder," said the trooper pointing to the cart.

George stepped up to the vehicle and looked in. What he saw was the outline of a human figure stretched beneath a piece of coarse canvas. He drew back with a start.

"Who is it?"

The young trooper brought his horse to the side of the dray and lifted the covering from the face. Vincent, leaning forward, uttered a great cry, for the face he looked upon was Kitty's, but oh, so dreadfully changed, so altered.

"Where—where did you find her?"

"About four miles down the creek."

"And you think it's murder?"

"Devil a doubt of it. Here, look," and he pulled the covering back still further, "here are the finger-marks about her throat—as plain as though they had been pressed in putty. And, you see, the third finger of the left hand is missing. If there is any man at Dead Man's Flat with such a hand I wouldn't care to be in his shoes." And with a smile which might have meant anything he re-covered that once lovely face and the sad procession passed on.

George stood staring after it, utterly bewildered. Kitty murdered—the queenly, beautiful Kitty! It was too horrible. Yet, as the trooper had said, there could be no doubt of that. Here was a tragedy, indeed! It then was she to whom Smith alluded when he expressed sorrow for the woman. Her husband, jealous and furious at the trick she had played him, had sought this revenge; but, in his manner of doing it, had betrayed himself completely, for there must have been hundreds of people on the diggings who knew that the third finger of Mr. Peter Logan's left hand was missing.

And yet there was danger in his apprehension too. Should he tell the story of the cipher, what trouble might not arise through police officiousness? The tale would then become public property, and

George himself would be subjected to the strictest surveillance, the treasure confiscated, and the girl of his heart as far beyond his reach as ever.

Now, this is a selfish world, and humanity a singularly selfish product, as it could scarcely help being. Self very naturally comes foremost in all considerations, and Mr. Vincent was no exception to this universal rule. His life seemed so inseparably bound up with Edith's that the mere idea of parting with her made him feel ready to rebel against the whole world. Moreover, he had battled long in poverty and wretchedness, and he had no intention of losing his chance of happiness if he could preserve it. Though virtue may be its own reward, it is usually of such a trivial nature that men ignore it. Indeed, the market value of that excellent article is deplorably low.

Vincent was not one to linger, having

once made up his mind. He breakfasted hastily from some cold meat; got a fellow to look after the tent during his absence, and then set out for the town.

It was not much after seven when he pulled up at the "Emu's Head," but early as it was the place was already opened, and Edith, with a duster in one hand and a brush in the other, met him in the passage.

"George," she cried. "You—so early!"

"Yes, dear, I have come to take you away. This is no fit place for you. Drop that infernal brush." And as he spoke he took that inoffensive article from her and savagely threw it to the far end of the passage.

"What is the matter, George? You look quite pale and excited."

"Do I? Well, I will tell you presently. In the meantime, darling, go to your room and get ready to come with me."

"But I cannot leave the place like this,"

she cried. " Kitty is away somewhere, and I must wait till she comes back."

" I don't think she will come back," he said.

" What do you mean ? " asked the girl eagerly. " Is anything the matter ? "

" Yes, darling, much, much. You shall know all presently. By the way, is Logan in ? "

" I think so."

" Then go, dear. In five minutes I shall expect you."

She hesitated for a moment, then, blushing, said :

" Ought I to go like this ? "

" Won't you trust me ? "

" Ah, forgive me," she cried, the tears rushing to her eyes. Her arms went round his neck and she pressed her sweet mouth to his. The next moment she was gone.

With a quick step Vincent turned to

Logan's room, and reaching the door knocked loudly thereon.

"Who's there?" asked the landlord in a quivering voice.

"I—Vincent."

"What do you want?"

"I have come to tell you that they have discovered your wife's body."

"What! Has she made away with herself?"

"The police believe she has been murdered."

"Indeed. And what reason have they for believing so?"

"There are certain proofs which cannot be doubted."

Vincent heard him gasp in spite of the door between them. "Is that all?"

"It is enough," said George slowly, and with due emphasis. "The man who murdered her had the third finger of his left hand missing."

"How—how do you know that?"

"Because the marks are on her throat. The police may be here at any moment."

Logan never answered, but Vincent heard him mutter beneath his breath, and he also thought he heard him sink to the floor. But, having done all that he intended, the young fellow turned from the room and took up his stand in the passage, where, a few minutes later, he was joined by Edith.

"Where do we go?" she asked.

"I will take you round to the Bank," he said. "The new manager was a school-chum of mine, and I daresay he'll be glad to see me. He doesn't know I'm down to this, but he wasn't a bad sort of fellow. Then," he continued softly, the sudden sweetness of his voice making her quiver, "if—if you wouldn't mind doing it at a registry-office—or—or in a private room."

He stopped, embarrassed, gazing down into her dear eyes with an imploring look. She met his beseeching glance with a loving, trustful look; a sweet pink flush spread itself over her delicate face.

"It shall be as you wish," she said, and hid her burning face on his breast. He drew her tightly to him, kissing her fondly.

"Darling, darling," was all that he could say.

And so they went forth from the precincts of the "Emu's Head," and that was the last time Edith ever crossed its threshold.

His friend the banker received his old schoolfellow with open arms, and insisted upon George quitting the camp at once.

"We have plenty of room for you here," he said cheerily, "and here you shall be married this very day. Go you back to the camp and bring on all your baggage:

Maggie, my dear"—this to his wife, a pleasant-looking little woman—" you'll look after Miss Leslie, won't you? I'll go at once and hunt up a parson." And he immediately quitted the room on matrimonial thoughts intent. George, however, was after him, and before he reached the door placed a hand upon his shoulder.

"Just one moment, Frank," he said. "I have something to tell you." And taking the banker aside he told him in a few brief words the more salient points of this our chronicle of Dead Man's Flat.

"So you have found Hall's Plant, eh? Well, what a surprising story. By Jove, you're a lucky dog."

"Undoubtedly." But George was thinking of a greater treasure than that which the bushranger had hidden.

That same afternoon, after George had visited the camp and brought away his treasure, he and Edith were united in the bonds of wedlock by a gentleman who droned the solemn and beautiful service with a delightful Scotch accent. The place was the neat little drawing-room of the banker, the witnesses, the banker and his pleasant-faced wife. Edith had put on a soft white dress especially for the occasion, and if she wasn't the sweetest little woman a man ever pledged himself to cherish and protect, Mr. George Vincent was no judge of feminine beauty.

But while all this was going on in one part of the town, a detachment of half-a-dozen police marched up to the " Emu's Head," which they immediately entered, as though their mode of procedure had already been agreed upon. One, stepping into the bar, took up a position against the door, where he stood stolidly staring at the gentlemen who were then indulging in the agreeable process of refreshing the inner man; two others made for the back part of the establishment, while the chief of the three that remained called the individual who was behind the bar and requested, in somewhat peremptory tones, to be conducted to Mr. Logan.

"Mr. Logan is in his room, sir," said the man. "He has been there all day. What's he wanted for?"

"That's none of your business," was the Inspector's reply, keeping up the official reputation for politeness. "Where's his room?"

"The second one on the left."

The officers advanced to the room in question and the Inspector knocked loudly upon the door, but received no answer. Twice, three times he knocked, with a like result. Then he cried out, "Open, in the name of the law." But receiving no reply to this, he turned to his companions. "Break down the door, men."

In a moment one of the burliest banged his huge shoulder against the frail partition, and back it flew into a thousand splinters. Into the room the officers rushed *en masse*, expecting opposition, but they encountered instead the lifeless body of the landlord. It was stretched out on its face on the floor, and though a loaded revolver was found beside it, there was no trace of murder or suicide. In fact, Flash Jim, as he had once been called—in the days of which we have not written—being fat and weak of heart, had died through the stoppage of the heart's action, consequent upon the obese nature of his body and the fright and excitement through which he had lately gone.

George and Edith have now a charming villa at St. Kilda, and live in very agreeable style, doubly so to him, for has he not the loveliest wife in the place (ask him) and two perfectly beautiful children? Moreover, he is no longer haunted by the ghost of a pen, and no more he dreads the sight of a ponderous ledger. These are little things at which he often laughs now, for has he not, by judicious speculation, doubled the treasure he found at Dead Man's Flat? As soon as the children are big enough to undertake the journey, he intends to set out on a lengthened trip to Europe, for he has not forgotten the old aspirations of one who is now dearer to him than life. In the meantime, as if to prepare them for the great sea journey, he sails them daily in his little yacht, or strolls with them along the sand, and has even been known to build castles and dabble in sand pies—though what this last proceeding has to do with their initiation into the mysteries of sea life, no one knows but himself.

And in all these gentle wanderings they are invariably accompanied by a tall, handsome girl of some fourteen summers, whose great brown eyes are as full of honesty as one of the nobler animal's. We saw such eyes before, once before, and they belonged to a man who died away up at Dead Man's Flat; and when we inform you that this stately young lady's name is Miss Amelia Thomas, you may possibly connect her with the "little 'un" of whom the unfortunate Phil seemed so proud. George, true to his promise, had sought the wife of his late companion—sought and found her dead. Poverty and ill-health had proved too strong for her, and she succumbed, leaving her child to the tender mercies of the world. That child he, discovering, took back with him to his own home. Ever since then she has been to them as a daughter; and if you only had time to make her better acquaintance, you would be charmed with her culture and her grace, her sweet voice, her great earnest eyes, and above all by that devotion which she bears for her new father and mother.

THE END.

www.ingramcontent.com/pod-product-compliance
Lightning Source LLC
Chambersburg PA
CBHW021802230426
43669CB00008B/605